FELICIA CARTRIGHT

AND THE CASE OF THE
TWISTED KEY

Felicia   Joan

FELICIA CARTRIGHT
AND THE CASE OF THE
TWISTED KEY

BERNARD PALMER

ANEKO PRESS

Aneko Press Youth

www.anekopress.com

Aneko Press, Life Sentence Publishing, and our logos are trademarks of Life Sentence Publishing, Inc.
203 E. Birch Street
P.O. Box 652
Abbotsford, WI 54405

JUVENILE FICTION / Religious / Christian / Action & Adventure

Paperback ISBN: 979-8-88936-292-0

eBook ISBN: 979-8-88936-293-7

10   9   8   7   6   5   4   3   2   1

Available where books are sold

CONTENTS

Ch. 1: A Small Metal Object 1

Ch. 2: What's Going On? 9

Ch. 3: The Missing Key 17

Ch. 4: "I'm Scared!" 25

Ch. 5: The Little Tin Box 35

Ch. 6: A Splash 45

Ch. 7: A Daring Plan 55

Ch. 8: A Locked Door 63

Ch. 9: Footprints! 71

Ch. 10: A Stalled Engine 83

Ch. 11: The Key Fits! 93

Ch. 12: The Cut Rope Ladder 105

CHAPTER 1

A SMALL METAL OBJECT

Felicia Cartright leaned against the rail of the *Lori June* and stared dreamily over the quiet waters of the Gulf. The wind had ceased with the setting of the sun, but long, gentle swells marched silently across its line of vision. Most of them were smooth and unbroken, but now and again a sudden burst of air would go skipping erratically across the weakening seas. When that happened, the placid surface dimpled and a handful of diamonds danced fleetingly from the crest of one wave to another.

Felicia's soft blond hair tumbled unnoticed about her delicately featured face, and her lips parted slightly.

"Beautiful, isn't it?" a voice asked at her elbow. She started suddenly. She was so completely lost in the scene before her that she had not heard anyone come up.

"Oh, Mr. Chandler!" she exclaimed. "You startled me!"

He moved to the rail beside her and leaned against it. He was the quiet, dark-faced owner of the *Lori June*, who had so unexpectedly invited Felicia and Joan to make the voyage to Guatemala before school started that fall.

For several minutes Mr. Chandler also stared out to sea. Only he just gave the illusion of inattention. His lithe, muscular body was alert and tense, and his head was cocked slightly. He was listening. Listening intently.

All of that Felicia saw at a glance.

"Is something wrong?" she asked simply.

"Something wrong?" he echoed. His jaw snapped firmly, and his manner grew stern. "Something wrong? Of course not. What could possibly go wrong?"

He turned to face her and was smiling curiously.

"What makes you think there's something wrong?" he persisted.

Embarrassment gripped her. "It's probably just my imagination," she finished lamely, "but it seemed to me just now that you were listening *to* something or listening *for* something."

He laughed his admiration. "I might have known I couldn't fool a young lady," he said easily. "As a matter of fact, I have the annoying habit of listening to the hum of the engines when we're out to sea. It's a carry over from my tour of duty on a destroyer, I guess."

He took a small metal object from his pocket and began to finger it subconsciously.

"Having a good time?" he asked after a moment or two.

"Wonderful!" Felicia exclaimed a bit breathlessly. "I still have trouble, though, believing that we're actually on a yacht bound for Guatemala."

He flipped the key into the air and deftly caught it again.

"You'll believe it tomorrow, Felicia," he said. "We'll be there in the morning."

She shifted uncertainly, and, for an instant, stared beyond the owner of the *Lori June*.

"Have you gotten acquainted with Mimi yet?" he asked.

Felicia paused. Of course she had gotten acquainted with Miriam (Mimi) Graham. There were only a handful of people aboard. The girls could not have missed knowing one another.

"We were introduced the first day, and this afternoon we played deck tennis together."

"I know that," he insisted. "But have you gotten acquainted with her? Do you know her?"

Felicia thought for a minute.

"No," she answered truthfully, "I don't think I know her at all."

He chuckled mirthlessly and returned the key to his pocket.

"I'm not surprised," he said. "I've been around

her for ten years, and I still don't know her." He breathed deeply. "You're aware, of course, that she is Phoebe's niece."

Felicia nodded.

"Your wife told Joan and me about Mimi the afternoon we left Boston."

"Phoebe seems to think she is our responsibility." He raised an eyebrow expressively. "She says we've got to help get her straightened out." He clasped the railing and tightened his grip on it until his knuckles showed white. "If she can be straightened out."

Felicia did not answer immediately, but when she did, her voice was firm and clear.

"What Mimi needs is to see that her life has no meaning apart from Jesus Christ," she said. "He is the only One who can help her or any of us."

The handsome, gray-haired Mr. Chandler had been relaxed as they talked. Now he jerked around, his very manner bristling.

"That's all we need!" he muttered pointedly. "A good, stiff dose of some fanatical religion to scramble that mixed-up kid's thinking a little more." The friendliness had gone out of his voice.

"But–" Felicia tried to protest.

However, he turned on his heel abruptly and strode across the deck, leaving her standing there.

She was still standing there, motionless, when Joan Bailey came up.

"Now what are you doing out here by yourself?"

Joan asked. "Speak quickly, and remember, anything you say may be used against you."

But Felicia scarcely noticed her.

"I'm afraid I made Mr. Chandler awfully angry just now," she said.

"I'm the one who usually says things I don't mean," Joan went on, "and gets people upset."

"That's just it," Felicia told her thoughtfully. "I really didn't say anything at all. He was talking with me about Mimi and how much she needed help. I told him that I knew Jesus could help her if she would confess her sin and trust Him as her Savior. And he blew up!"

Joan's face twisted with questions. "That is strange. Especially when he is such a good friend of Dr. and Mrs. Rawlins."

Felicia nodded.

Dr. and Mrs. Rawlins were a Christian couple. He taught archaeology at the university, and Mrs. Rawlins taught English at Wellington School for Girls. They were the ones who had been instrumental in getting Felicia and Joan invited to make the late summer cruise.

"I cannot understand it, Joan," Felicia repeated. "One minute he was as friendly and agreeable as anyone I've ever met. The next he was in a cold rage."

Joan expelled her breath slowly.

"It doesn't sound like him," she admitted. "I mean it doesn't seem to be the sort of thing he would say."

Felicia shivered.

"You should have seen the look in his eyes. I don't know when I've seen anyone so angry."

Felicia Cartright turned back to the rail. The wind was freshening, and the breakers were broad and deep-throated. Clouds had stolen in silently to cloak the stars. In that moment, it seemed that the *Lori June* was moving through a thick, impenetrable shroud.

"Does Mimi seem to be as bad as he says she is?" Joan asked after a time.

"She's quiet," Felicia replied, "and a little distant, but that's all I have noticed about her."

Joan would have replied but stopped abruptly as the door to the lounge opened. A yellow shaft of light illuminated the girls' faces briefly before the door swung shut once more.

"Hello, Connie," Felicia said smiling.

Connie Adams was the daughter of the *Lori June*'s captain. A vivacious, bright-eyed girl, she liked Felicia and Joan immediately.

"I thought I'd find you out here," she said. "Hasn't this been a lovely night?"

"Until it got so cloudy and dark," Felicia added.

"The clouds will be gone in a few minutes," Connie told them. "They always come and go down here at this time of year. And if it does rain, it's only for a few minutes. I think that's one of the reasons I like it so well."

She stopped speaking suddenly. Her tiny, young figure stiffened.

"Did you see anything at that hatch just now?" she asked in a hoarse whisper.

"You mean that door?" Joan asked.

"Yes," Connie said, nodding vigorously, "at that hatch."

"It certainly wasn't anything to be alarmed about," Joan said crisply. "It was just one of the sailors. He stood there a minute or so to get some fresh air."

"That's just what I thought I saw," she exclaimed. "The hands aren't supposed to be up here. At least not when they are off duty."

"Maybe your dad gave him permission to come up," Felicia put in almost hopefully.

"No," Connie repeated, "he wouldn't do that." She grasped Joan and Felicia by the arms. "I–I'm worried."

"I don't know what there is to be worried about," Joan answered. "We have no money for him to steal."

Connie moved backward noiselessly and motioned for them to join her. "Come over here," she whispered. "I've got to tell you something."

She led them to an inconspicuous corner on the deck.

"When the time came for us to sail, two of Dad's best men were missing," she said. "He had to go out on the wharf and pick up a couple of guys who were loafing there."

Felicia's face was strained and drawn. "Is that bad?" she asked.

Connie nodded. "It could be," she said cryptically. "But there's something worse. The *Lori June*'s radio operator picked up a strange radio signal this morning."

"What does that mean?" the girls demanded.

"The operator seldom uses the radio in midmorning if the weather is good, but he happened to do so today. He picked up a signal that was loud and clear."

"We passed quite a few boats today," Joan reminded her. "It could have been one of those, or it could have been a freak signal. That happens."

"There were no boats in the area at that particular time," Connie whispered, "yet the signal came in as clearly as though it were being broadcast from the house next door." She bit her lower lip to keep it from trembling. "Dad and the crew tore the *Lori June* upside down looking for a radio-sending set and couldn't find it," Connie went on. "But he and the operator are still convinced that someone has it aboard!"

"But why?" Felicia asked.

"That," Connie replied, only forming the words with her lips, "is something we do not know."

CHAPTER 2

WHAT'S GOING ON?

Connie Adams pursed her lips tightly, as though she had already said more than she should have said and turned her attention to the night about them.

"See," she said, changing the subject, "it's not going to rain after all."

"I was just thinking that myself," Joan Bailey replied.

The clouds had been swept away to reveal a million pinpricks of light in the soft, blue sky, and the moon, pushing majestically above the horizon, cast a long, silvery path across the water. The wind, weary of playing tag over the crystal water, yawned once or twice to cause a brief flurry of waves and tiptoed silently to bed. The only sound was the vibrant throbbing of the engines, and even they seemed muted and subdued.

Felicia shook away the spell that the beauty of the night was casting on her and turned to Connie.

Her lips parted, and she moistened them with the tip of her tongue.

"Connie," she said at last.

The other girl looked at her and glanced quickly away.

"Why would anyone aboard the *Lori June* want to hide a radio transmitter?" Felicia asked softly.

Connie Adams stiffened. "Forget that I told you anything about that transmitter," she whispered.

One moment passed and then another. Connie's face was twitching nervously.

"But why?" Felicia persisted.

For answer their new friend turned and walked hurriedly away.

Joan expelled her breath sharply. "Now what do you suppose is the matter with her?" she said.

Felicia took a step forward, involuntarily, almost as though she were going to follow Connie.

"There's something going on here," the Cartright girl said at last. "Something you and I aren't supposed to know anything about."

"But Connie knows," Joan repeated thoughtfully. "Is that it?"

"She knows more than we do."

They went silently down to their stateroom and bolted the door securely.

Joan Bailey shuddered.

"All of a sudden, this yacht is giving me the willies," she said.

Felicia managed a weak smile. "I'm certainly glad there's a lock on our door tonight."

Joan dropped nervously to the side of the bed. Her dark eyes were moving continuously, as though alert for some intruder.

"I've had the strangest feeling about this trip," she said, her voice growing softer, "ever since Dr. and Mrs. Rawlins invited us to go along with them and the Chandlers."

"I know," Felicia admitted.

It had seemed strange to both of them that the English instructor from Wellington School for Girls and her professor husband were friendly enough with the Chandlers to invite guests along for a summer cruise on the Chandler yacht. And even stranger that they had been selected, although it had not seemed too unusual at the time.

"Come to think of it," Felicia continued, "Mrs. Rawlins was never particularly close to us."

"She was close to me," Joan pointed out quickly, an impish grin twisting her face. "Why I spent more time in consultation with Mrs. Rawlins than any other girl at school."

"You wouldn't have," Felicia reminded her, "if you had your assignments in on time."

"I think she gave me extra long assignments purposely," Joan announced, her eyes dancing but her manner serious, "just so I would spend time with her."

Felicia picked up a book from the dresser and began to flip through it absent-mindedly.

"The way I see it," Joan went on, "there's got to be a reason for this trip. There's got to be some good, solid reason why they wanted us to come along instead of anyone else. If there weren't, they wouldn't have asked us."

"There was a reason for asking us," Felicia reminded her. "Remember Mrs. Rawlins told us about Mimi Graham's mother dying and how the Chandlers wanted us along for company for her. They thought we would be good for her."

"I know they told us that," Joan repeated, "and I believed them, but now I'm not so sure. Connie is aboard, and Mimi has spent more time with her than she has with us. They haven't needed you and me to be companions to her."

Felicia picked up her comb and brush and laid them down again.

"I know Mr. Chandler talked with us about her a few minutes ago," Joan continued, "but he didn't sound too convincing to me."

The Cartright girl's forehead wrinkled.

"You make it sound so–so mysterious – so frightening." A sudden chill danced up her spine.

Joan got hurriedly to her feet and went over to Felicia.

"There are some strange things going on," she whispered, "if you ask me. Some very strange things."

"There may be a perfectly logical explanation for them. That radio transmitter everyone is so excited about could be located a thousand miles away. Atmospheric conditions can play weird tricks."

Joan breathed deeply. "Maybe," she said. "Maybe not. Let's think back to the very beginning."

Felicia turned and leaned against the dresser. "Yes?"

"We were asked to make this cruise at the last minute, weren't we? And we were cautioned to say nothing to anyone else at Wellington about the trip."

"That was so the other girls wouldn't be jealous," Felicia said quietly.

Her friend's eyes darkened.

"That is what you and I were told," Joan continued. "But was that the real reason? *Was it?*"

Felicia laughed nervously.

"You sound like Sherlock Holmes."

"When we got on board the *Lori June*," Joan continued, ignoring Felicia's remark, "we found that everyone else had known for several weeks about the cruise and where we were going. In fact, no one seemed surprised that we were along."

"I know all those things, Joan," Felicia replied, "and I've done some thinking about them, but I have confidence in Dr. and Mrs. Rawlins, and the Chandlers seem like lovely people. I do not believe they would be a party to anything wrong."

"I don't either," Joan said. "At least I didn't. But there is something going on that we're not supposed to know anything about. All of these things just couldn't happen without some reason for them."

"You saw the equipment Dr. Rawlins brought aboard," Felicia reminded her crisply, "and you know he's an archaeologist. He's probably talked Mr. Chandler into taking him to some new spot to do some excavating. And if that's what it is, we're going to feel mighty silly."

Joan nodded.

"If that is all it is," she said, "you may be right." She lowered her voice then. "But that explanation does not answer a lot of questions I have. Why all the secrecy? And why didn't we stop at Miami so Mrs. Rawlins and Mrs. Chandler could do their shopping? Why did we have to keep pushing on? And why did those two men quit just before sailing time? Was it because they got wind of something that the *Lori June* is to do? Were they afraid?"

Felicia Cartright was a long while in speaking. She, too, had been vaguely disturbed by the cruise of the *Lori June*. But her fears were vague and indistinct; a sort of suspicion and dread that could not be put into words.

Joan returned to the big easy chair in the far corner of their stateroom and dropped into it easily.

"Oh, well," she said, "worrying won't get us anywhere!"

"No," Felicia answered, "but you've got me doing a lot of thinking. What *is* going on?"

Joan stood nervously. "The thing that concerns me is not knowing," she said. "We've just got to find out."

Felicia sighed wearily.

"Let's have our devotions and turn in," she said at last. "Maybe things won't seem so bad tomorrow."

It was Joan's time to have devotions. She read a chapter from the New Testament, and both girls knelt to pray.

Felicia thought she would not sleep at all, but she drifted off almost immediately, and it seemed like the next minute, the raucous jangling of the alarm awakened her.

"Now," Joan said, swinging her feet over the side of the bed and sitting up, "that is just about the shortest night on record. I don't think I even had time to close my eyes."

"I thought you weren't going to close your eyes until we got safely back to port," Felicia told her.

"That's what I had decided," Joan retorted. "Then I figured that if anything terrible were going to happen, it would be much easier if it happened while we were asleep. Besides, I was dog-tired. I just couldn't stay awake."

The girls dressed rapidly.

"How do you feel this morning, Joan?" Felicia called from the adjoining dressing room.

"Like a little girl," Joan said sheepishly, "who has just realized that she's almost frightened herself to death with her own ghost stories."

Felicia grinned.

"That's exactly the way I feel," she said. "Somehow things don't seem to be so bad in daytime."

Joan paused, her hand on the door.

"Only it isn't going to stay daylight all the time on this cruise," she said. "It's going to get dark again."

"Come on," Felicia said, hurrying her out of the door. "I'm not going to let you get me afraid of my own shadow again this morning."

Yet, as they entered the dining room, Felicia could not help wondering. Everyone seemed to be laughing happily. But was the laughter genuine? Or was it veneer to hide some serious, almost illegal purpose? For an instant, it seemed as though a chilly blast of Arctic air swept over her. She shivered in the force of it. Then it was gone, and the dining room was warm again.

"There's Mimi," Joan exclaimed, brightening. "Let's have breakfast with her."

She would have moved to the table immediately, but Felicia hung back. She eyed the girl who was sitting there.

"Wait," she whispered in Joan's ear.

"But why? Don't you want to make friends with her?"

Felicia nodded. "But I wonder if we should go over there right now. She's been crying."

CHAPTER 3

THE MISSING KEY

For a brief instant, Felicia Cartright and Joan Bailey stood near the door, staring uneasily around the dining room. They had started to move toward the table where Mimi Graham was sitting, and everyone had noticed them. Now they could feel the eyes of others on them.

Joan turned toward another table, but Felicia grasped her, inconspicuously, by the sleeve.

Mimi had glanced up at them. Her lips trembled uncertainly, and her gaze wavered. She tried hard to smile but could not. Instead, she coughed and hid her face behind her napkin.

"She's seen us now," Felicia whispered to Joan, "and everyone knows that we were heading for her table. We've got to go and sit with her."

They moved leisurely toward the table, laughing and talking as they went.

"Hi," Joan said, smiling brightly.

Mimi managed to speak, but she did not look at the girls.

"We didn't expect to see you at breakfast so early," Felicia said, pulling out a chair and sitting down.

"I've been up for hours." She spoke without emotion, but there was sadness in her eyes and in the lines about her youthful mouth. Mimi was a small girl, as her nickname suggested, and fine-featured. An attractive, vivacious brunette who would have seemed much more suited to laughter than to tears. Yet Felicia and Joan had never seen her smile.

For a moment or two, the silence was awkward. Felicia picked up the folder with the choices for breakfast listed.

"What are you having for breakfast, Mimi?" she asked. "I'm almost starved."

"Some toast and coffee," the other girl answered.

"Know what I'm going to do?" Joan broke in. "I'm going to tell the steward to surprise me. I like surprises."

"At breakfast?" Felicia asked, wrinkling her nose.

"Especially at breakfast."

"You may get more of a surprise than you ask for," the Cartright girl went on. "He may bring you some barbecued octopus tentacles or raw Conch on the half shell."

Joan shuddered.

"You always ruin everything," she bantered.

"The trouble with you, Joan," Felicia told her, "is that you have no imagination. You don't see where something like that can lead."

"I take it back," Joan assured her. "I take it back. From now on, I'm strictly a bacon-and-eggs-for-breakfast girl."

The corners of Mimi's mouth lifted slightly. But only for a moment.

"The steward told us yesterday that we ought to get where we're going sometime this morning," Felicia said.

Mimi nodded. "That's what Uncle Norris told me yesterday."

"But tell me," Joan put in, "are we there? And if we are, where are we?"

Mimi laughed briefly, in spite of herself.

"You sound confused," she said.

"Confused?" Joan echoed. "Both Felicia and I are downright bewildered. We don't know anything except that we're supposed to be making a cruise to Central America."

Before she paused for breath, Connie Adams joined them.

"Are you still talking, Joan?" she asked. "I thought you ran down last night."

Joan made a face at her, impishly. "I thought you were my friend," she said.

"Joan hasn't run down since I've known her," Felicia countered, "and that's been three years."

Connie pulled up a chair and sat down.

"Maybe you can tell us about where we are," Felicia said when Connie had given her order to the steward.

"I just came from the bridge," Connie replied. "Dad says that we ought to reach our destination off the coast of Guatemala in an hour or so."

The party at a nearby table had gotten to their feet and was leaving. Felicia did not notice them until she heard Mr. Chandler speak almost at her elbow.

"But I tell you I had it a few minutes ago," he said.

Mrs. Chandler turned back to him.

"What is it, Norris?" she asked.

He was staring intently at the deck. "Just a little key," he mumbled as though it were not especially important. "I know I had it this morning."

"What sort of key was it?"

"Just a little key," he said, spacing his fingers to indicate its length. "I must have dropped it in the stateroom. I'll go and see."

"Why don't you let it go?" she asked, her voice rising slightly. "We haven't got anything valuable aboard that we have to keep under a lock. And besides, there's no one aboard who would steal."

"I know that," he said, "but I've got to find it just the same. The rest of you go out on deck. I'll go back to our stateroom and see if I left it there."

"All right," his wife answered, "but hurry."

His gaze met Felicia's quite by chance. There was concern in his eyes. Concern that was not quite hidden by the smile on his lips.

"Did you girls happen to see a little key?" he asked casually.

"We saw you playing with one last night," Felicia told him. "You were tossing it in the air and catching it."

"I remember that," he said. "And I was sure I had it this morning, too. It must be in our cabin."

No one at the girls' table spoke until Mr. Chandler had left the room.

"He seems awfully excited about that key, doesn't he?" Joan asked.

"Only," Felicia added, "he doesn't want anyone to know that he's excited and worried about it."

"I can't figure out what the fuss is all about," Connie said. "I've seen Mr. Chandler playing with that key lots of times. It's just a little, sort of twisted, key. It doesn't look as though it would unlock anything."

"I just thought of something," Joan said. "We all knew about the key. We'd seen Mr. Chandler juggling it. Why hadn't his wife seen it?"

"Oh, she had!" Mimi broke in quickly. "She's seen it lots of times." She stopped and her face flushed crimson. "I–I mean–" For the moment she could not speak.

"It doesn't matter," Felicia said. "We shouldn't be talking about Mr. Chandler anyway. He–"

Mimi's throat constricted. She swallowed hard, and the tears welled in her eyes.

Just then the steward brought their breakfasts, and they ate in silence. Now and again, someone made a feeble effort at conversation, but it sputtered dismally.

"Now remember," Connie said when they had finished eating, "we're all going swimming as soon as we drop anchor. That's the thing I've been waiting for. You've never seen such sparkling, clean water! And so warm! It's positively out of this world!"

"Just say the word," Joan told her. "It sounds wonderful to me."

They left the dining room together. Felicia would have followed her roommate back to their stateroom, but Mimi Graham touched her lightly on the arm and motioned her to one side.

The Cartright girl smiled and nodded.

"I'll see you in a little while, Joan," she said aloud.

Felicia and Mimi went out to the rail and looked across the long, rolling waves. For several minutes neither spoke.

"Joan and I have been so grateful to your uncle and aunt, Mimi," she said at last, "for asking us to make the trip with you."

"They wanted you along because of me, didn't they?" Mimi asked. She shot out the hard, accusing words.

"What makes you say that?" Felicia parried.

"Didn't they?" Mimi insisted.

"They thought it would be good for you to have someone your own age along," Felicia said. "Especially after the shock and sorrow you have gone through."

Mimi's small face grew iron hard.

"I don't need you or anyone else around me," she said almost angrily. "I can take care of myself."

Felicia was so shocked, so stunned by the onslaught of words that she could say nothing. Mimi started to leave but came back and lowered her voice.

"I don't know why Aunt Phoebe pretended not to know about that twisted key," she whispered. "But she knew all about it. She's seen it hundreds of times."

Joan Bailey could scarcely believe it when Felicia told her what had happened.

"But that doesn't sound like Mimi at all," she said. "She's not that sort of person."

"We don't think she's that sort of person," Felicia replied, "but actually we don't know. We've only been with her a little while."

"I know that," Joan said loyally, "but I still think there must be a reason for what Mimi did just now."

"The poor kid is beside herself with grief for her mother," Felicia added. "That's part of the trouble."

"And she doesn't know Jesus as her Savior. Just think how terrible it would be to lose a loved one and not have assurance of heaven!"

Felicia was slow in answering.

"You make me awfully ashamed, Joan," she said at last. "I didn't once try to witness to her. Maybe if I had–"

In an hour or so, the *Lori June* dropped anchor. Almost immediately, Connie came running down to their stateroom and hammered on the door.

"Get into those swimsuits!" she sang out. "Time's wasting!"

Felicia was surprised when they got on deck and saw Mimi already there. She was quiet and pensive, but in spite of that, she seemed to enjoy herself.

They swam for an hour or more in the sun-drenched water off the Guatemalan coast. It was all that Connie said it was and more. The Gulf was clear and clean and filled with thousands of dainty, multicolored tropical fish. There were sea fans and fantastic spires and ledges of coral in many hues.

The girls went skin diving from one of the lifeboats, bringing up conch shells, sea fans, and exciting bits of coral and shell life.

It scarcely seemed possible that the afternoon was gone when the captain called them aboard with an imperious blast of the foghorn.

Dr. Rawlins and Mr. Chandler were waiting on deck for them.

"Well," the yacht owner said, "did you have a good time?"

He asked Mimi, but it was Joan who answered.

"Wonderful," she said. And then she noticed something in his hand.

"I see you found your key," she said.

A strange look crossed his face.

"The key? Oh–oh, yes!" He laughed sheepishly. "I found it in our stateroom this afternoon."

CHAPTER 4

"I'M SCARED!"

On the trip south, most of the group aboard the yacht, with one or two exceptions, had been in a gala mood. Felicia and Joan had seemed alone in their concern over what might happen, concern that ebbed and flowed within them capriciously.

There were games going on constantly in the lounge and on deck; games that often lasted until one or two o'clock in the morning, simply because no one was ready to go to bed. The evenings were calm and warm and beautiful, an almost irresistible lure for deck walking or lazing dreamily in a chair at the rail.

Sleep was a phenomenon that belonged to another world, another era; one of the burdens of less fortunate people who could not laze the days away. Such was the complete detachment from the things about them.

But now that the *Lori June* had reached her

destination, it was different. The change came about subtly, but unmistakably. There was a taut, expectant attitude aboard the yacht, a quickening tempo that seemed to sharpen and accentuate every action, every chance remark.

Felicia felt it as she and Joan entered the dining room that evening. It was present suddenly and without warning; a vague, indistinct feeling of tension and dread, the chill breath of apprehension that started her shivering. In an instant, the doubts, the nameless forebodings that had come now and again the past few days, rushed in as though to overwhelm her.

She looked about and shuddered.

"Felicia," Joan whispered, "you've got goose bumps. Are you cold?"

She shook her head.

"Hi," Connie Adams sang out from a table toward the rear. "Come on over. We've been waiting for you."

Felicia shook off her fears and managed a smile.

"Here we are late again," she said, "and I thought we were going to be early for a change."

"I've never been so hungry," Connie said. "There's something about swimming that makes me ravenous."

"Me, too," Joan put in.

Felicia glanced at Mimi Graham. She was staring into her plate unsmilingly. A tear trembled uncertainly at the corner of her eye. Impulsively, Felicia laid a hand on her arm.

"Mimi," she said softly, her voice tender, "is there something wrong?"

For a long minute the other girl did not look up. But when she did, her eyes were blazing.

"Why don't you leave me alone?" she blurted so loudly that everyone in the dining hall heard her.

Felicia gasped at the sudden onslaught.

"I–I'm sorry," she said lamely.

Mimi stared at her and at the other two girls at the table. Then she leaped to her feet and ran from the room.

"Now what was the matter with her?" Connie demanded when she could speak. "I've never seen her act like that before."

Joan shook her head.

"The poor girl," Felicia said gently. "She must be terribly upset." She pushed back from the table and got up. "I'll be back in a few minutes," she told them, mindful that everyone in the dining room was watching her. Her cheeks flushed daintily.

"Where are you going?" Joan asked.

"Go ahead and eat," Felicia said. "Don't wait for me."

The Cartright girl did not know exactly what she intended to do. Once outside the dining room, she paused and looked around. Darkness had already come, and the *Lori June* was rocking gently at anchor half a mile or so offshore.

Mimi may have gone to her stateroom, but somehow

Felicia did not think so. The chances were that she was walking the deck or staring down into the water. With a prayer in her heart, Felicia moved quietly along the deck. In the shadows near the bow, she saw a small figure at the rail. Her pulse quickened.

For a brief instant, she bowed her head.

"Lord Jesus," she prayed, "help me to know what to say to Mimi."

She went close enough to be sure that it was the Graham girl at the rail and stopped.

"It's beautiful tonight, isn't it?" she said.

There was no answer.

Felicia stepped closer.

"I'm terribly sorry I offended you just now, Mimi," she continued.

The other girl moved half a step away. When she spoke, her voice was hoarse and grating.

"Leave me alone."

Felicia leaned against the rail casually. "I've felt the way you do tonight," she acknowledged, just loud enough to be heard above the murmuring of the waves, "lots of times. I've felt that I didn't have a friend in the world; that there was no one who was truly interested in me."

Mimi's lips tightened.

"But that was before I knew Jesus Christ," she continued. "Before I acknowledged my sin and put my trust in Him."

The other girl turned to face Felicia. Her entire being trembled.

"Don't preach religion at me!" she exclaimed. "I can't stand it tonight!"

Felicia waited prayerfully.

"I'm not preaching religion to you, Mimi," she said after a time. "In fact, I'm not preaching to you at all. I'm simply telling you what Jesus has meant in my own life."

In the semi-darkness, Mimi stared at her curiously.

She gulped and ran her fingers nervously across her face.

"I shouldn't have exploded like that this evening," she said. "I know you meant only to help me." She sighed with a weariness that seemed to come from the very depths of her soul.

"Let's forget it, okay?" Felicia suggested smiling.

Mimi turned back to the water once more and stared downward, as though striving to plumb the impenetrable depths with her eyes.

"I don't have anyone who really cares about me," she continued. "I mean *really* cares."

"But you do," Felicia told her.

Mimi turned her attention back to Felicia. "Aunt Phoebe likes me," she said, "probably as much as anyone else, but she doesn't really care for me the way Mom did."

"I wasn't thinking about Aunt Phoebe. The Bible tells us that *God so loved the world* (that means you too, Mimi), *that He sent His only begotten Son, that whosoever believes on Him should not perish but have everlasting life.* He loved us so much that He sent Jesus to die on the cross for us. So never say that no one cares for you, Mimi."

A strange look came over the other girl's face.

"I've heard that verse, of course," she managed, "but I have never thought of it in quite that way."

She took out a tissue and dried her eyes. "I'm sorry I said what I did to you a little while ago," she said, changing the subject abruptly. "I was just upset."

"Let's forget it," Felicia told her. Together they went down to Mimi's stateroom.

"You go back and have dinner," she said.

"But what about you?"

"I'm not hungry," Mimi replied. "Besides, I couldn't go back into the dining room tonight. I look a mess."

"I'll be praying for you," Felicia assured her.

When she went back to the dining hall, Joan and Connie were still sitting at the table toying with their desserts.

"Is she all right?" Joan asked, her lips forming the words soundlessly.

Felicia nodded.

"She feels better now."

Connie rang for the steward.

"I told them to keep something warm for you," she said.

By this time the dining room was beginning to

empty. Mrs. Chandler stopped at their table on the way out.

"Thank you, Felicia," she murmured. "Thank you very much."

Dr. Rawlins, who was right behind her, glanced at his watch.

"You girls had better hurry," he said pointedly. "It's almost bedtime."

Joan looked at her own watch. "Why it's only eight o'clock," she protested.

He eyed her momentarily.

"We've got a big day ahead of us tomorrow," he went on. "We're all going to hit the hay right now, and I'd strongly advise you to do the same."

"I'm bushed from swimming," Connie said. "I think I'm going to turn in."

"I didn't do any swimming," Norris Chandler added, tossing the twisted key into the air and catching it absent-mindedly, "but I'm about all in just the same. I'm going to bed so I can be ready for those big sailfish tomorrow."

"Well, if everyone else aboard is going to bed early," Felicia said, "I suppose we'll have to do the same."

She chanced to be watching Dr. Rawlins as she spoke. The look in his eye bothered her. Was it actually relief that flashed across his impassive face?

Joan and Felicia went down to their stateroom when they had finished eating.

"I don't get it," Joan said. "All the way down here

no one has cared whether they ever went to bed or not. Now, all of a sudden, they're turning in almost before it gets dark. I don't get it."

Felicia took off her shoes.

"Did it seem to you that they were anxious to get you and me to go to bed too?" she asked.

"That's the thing that got me," the Bailey girl replied. "I haven't had so many people interested in getting me to bed since my big sister entertained her first boyfriend at home one evening."

Felicia laughed.

"Well, I guess it won't hurt us any," she said.

"But why do they want us in bed?" Joan insisted, her voice an intense whisper. "Did you ever think about that? Could it be they want us asleep, so we'll be out of the way? Do you suppose something is going on tonight? Something we don't know anything about?"

Felicia trembled slightly.

"I'd never thought of that," she said.

The girls had devotions together, switched out the lights, and crawled into bed.

"I don't think I'll be able to close my eyes all night," Felicia said under her breath.

"I will," Joan retorted firmly. "I'm going to *make* myself go to sleep. If anything's going on that we're not supposed to know about, I want to be sure and oblige them."

Felicia lay on her back, her eyes open. The port-hole was open, and the soft moonlight filtered in to dispel some of the blackness. She could see the chest of drawers in the corner and the closets along one bulkhead.

Everyone aboard must have gone to bed early. The *Lori June* was silent. Silent and almost motionless. What was this all about? What was going on? The questions coursed through Felicia's mind.

Half an hour passed, and she began to nod sleepily. Her eyelids grew heavy and almost closed. Whether or not she dropped off to sleep she did not know, but she awakened with a start.

Sweat beaded her forehead and her shoulders trembled.

For a moment or two she lay there breathing heavily. What was it that had awakened her? That feeling of dread and apprehension? The talk she had with Mimi?

And then she heard it once more. It was a subdued muffled sound, so faint and indistinct that she would have missed it at any other time except for the breathless silence that had enveloped the yacht.

Felicia raised on one elbow, straining every fiber to hear the sound again.

"Joan!" she hissed softly.

It had only been a whisper, but her roommate was awake instantly.

She heard the sound again, the guarded bumping of wood against iron.

"Did you hear that?" Felicia demanded.

Joan nodded tensely. "It–it sounds as though some-one is lowering something over the side," she said.

Felicia stole out of bed and crept to the porthole. She looked out.

"C-c-can you see anything?" Joan asked, her teeth chattering.

"Nothing but sky and water," Felicia whispered.

Even as she spoke, the sounds stopped abruptly, and all was silent once more.

Felicia Cartright did not move from the center of the stateroom for a time.

"Felicia," Joan said, *"I–I'm scared!"*

CHAPTER 5

THE LITTLE TIN BOX

Felicia Cartright and Joan Bailey huddled together in one of the twin beds and waited, praying for daylight. But it seemed that even time was against them. The minutes crawled by on hesitant, dragging feet, and the hours seemed not to move at all.

Dawn was long in coming.

Toward morning the wind freshened, and the *Lori June* strained noisily against the anchor chains as she began to roll with the breakers. A cloud must have crept over the moon, for the darkness increased suddenly.

"I don't like this," Joan whispered. "I'm going to turn on a light."

"We don't dare," Felicia replied. "We can't let anyone know that we're awake."

"Who would be up at this hour?"

"Maybe the same people who launched that boat

during the night," the Cartright girl answered, shuddering. "And if they see our light, they may guess that we heard."

Joan rolled over and sat up.

"Why do you suppose they left the yacht last night?" she asked curiously.

Felicia expelled her breath. "When we find the answer to that, we will have the answer to many things."

A minute passed while they listened to the rhythmic creaking of the anchor chains.

Joan got into her robe and slippers.

"Mr. Chandler did everything he could to trundle us off to bed last night right after dinner," she said thoughtfully. "Do you suppose that means anything?"

"It could have only been a coincidence."

"I suppose it could," Joan said after a time, "but too many things have happened for them *all* to be coincidences."

Felicia got up too. By this time, it was daylight, and further sleep was impossible.

"Did you hear anything else?" she asked her roommate.

"I don't really know," she replied truthfully. "I kept thinking I did, but I wasn't real sure."

They got up so early that it seemed the breakfast bell was sounded in the middle of the day.

"At last," Joan sighed, getting to her feet. "If I eat three breakfasts, you'll know why."

"Just be careful of what you say," Felicia warned her. "We can't let on that we heard anything."

"N-n-no one will get anything out of me," Joan whispered, rolling her eyes upward. "If they start to question me, I–I'll get so scared I won't even be able to talk."

In the dining hall, Mimi and Connie were sitting together at a table. They smiled and waved at Felicia and Joan as they stepped inside the door.

"Come on over," Connie called pleasantly. "We've been waiting for you."

Felicia studied Mimi as they approached. She was trying to smile, but her lips were tense, and her hands, resting on the table, were working nervously. She glanced up at Felicia. For an instant, her gaze hung there in something akin to desperation. Felicia started as she caught the look, and Mimi, suddenly flustered, turned quickly away.

"I'm so excited about today," Connie Adams said as soon as the other two were seated. "Dad talked with Mr. Chandler, and he's going to let us go fishing in the launch today."

"Fishing?" Felicia exclaimed. "Wonderful!"

Only Mimi's face twisted distastefully.

"What's the matter?" Joan asked her. "Don't you like to go fishing?"

"I never catch anything," Mimi said petulantly, "and besides, I couldn't bear to put worms on my hook."

"Worms?" Connie echoed, laughing good-naturedly. "You sound as though you need a couple of fishing lessons. In the first place, we don't use worms, and besides, the skipper baits our hooks for us. And in the second place, fishing is just about the most fun you ever had, especially if you happen to snag a marlin or a sailfish."

But Mimi was unconvinced.

"I don't see how you can get so excited about fishing at a time like this," she said in a hushed voice.

Felicia dropped her fork!

"Time like this?" she repeated. "W-w-what do you mean?"

Mimi leaned forward. "Didn't you hear a noise last night?" she asked.

The Cartright girl's eyes grew large and round.

"What sort of noise?" she managed.

Mimi picked up her glass and sipped the water nervously. Her slender fingers were trembling.

"This morning just before dawn," she whispered, "I heard someone in the passageway outside my stateroom."

"Are–are you sure?" Joan put in.

She nodded.

"I'm positive. I was as wide awake as I am right this minute. I heard those footsteps go down the passageway. Then I heard the door open that leads down to the hold!"

The girls were staring at one another wordlessly.

"For two or three minutes everything was quiet," she went on. "Then I heard the door open and close again, and the footsteps went back up the passageway."

Joan swallowed and moistened her lips.

"I–I don't like any of this," she said.

"There is no reason for us to get excited," Connie broke in calmly. "I don't know why anyone was going down the passageway to the hold in the middle of the night, but there must be a logical explanation. It was probably just one of the crew."

"But why would someone go down there in the middle of the night," Mimi insisted, "especially when hardly anyone ever goes down there during the day?"

Connie Adams changed the subject abruptly, a bit too abruptly to suit Felicia, and kept the conversation whirling until they had all finished breakfast.

"Oh!" she exclaimed suddenly, pushing back from the table and standing. "We'll have to hurry and get ready for the fishing expedition this morning. They like to leave about 9 o'clock."

"I–I don't think I'm going," Mimi said hesitantly.

"You ought to go," Felicia told her. "It won't be any fun for the rest of us if you don't."

There was a short pause.

"I don't have any clothes to wear," she protested lamely. "All I brought were good dresses."

"Come on down to our stateroom," Felicia said. "I think we can take care of that too."

"But I–"

"Go along with her, Mimi," Joan urged. "Between the two of us, I'm sure we've got some old clothes that will fit you." She stood and moved toward the door. "I'll see you in a little while."

"Going my way?" Connie asked her. "I'll walk along with you. I've got to change clothes too."

Joan shook her head. "I've got an errand to run," she explained. "I'll see you later."

She left the dining room quickly before Connie or one of the others decided to join her. Outside she paused and looked around casually. Captain Adams was on the bridge. She wouldn't have to worry about him. The Chandlers and the Rawlinses were in the dining room. They had just been served, and the way they were talking, it would be an hour before they finished breakfast. And the crew would be busy readying the launch.

Deciding suddenly, Joan turned and drummed a rapid staccato across the deck with her heels. It sounded above the fierce pounding of her heart. Her face and neck moistened noticeably, and she wet her lips with the tip of her tongue.

"Good morning, Miss Bailey," one of the crew said as they met in the passageway.

At the sound of his voice, she started.

"G-g-good morning," she managed.

She slipped inside her stateroom, took a small flashlight from under her pillow, and went out into the passageway once more. Mimi's stateroom was at the end of the passageway, next to the hatch that led below to the hold.

For an instant, Joan paused hesitantly. If someone saw her here, there would be no questions. But once she reached the hold, it would be different. Much different. What could she say if they caught her there?

She heard Felicia's voice! Her friend and Mimi were coming her way. That decided it for Joan. She whisked off her shoes, tiptoed along the passageway, and popped into the hatch that led down into the hold. And just in time. As the hatch closed behind her, Felicia and Mimi reached the lower deck.

For a moment or two, Joan Bailey was motionless. The girls were sure to hear her. Her heavy breathing would give her hiding place away. That or the fierce pounding of her heart. She shifted from one foot to the other. It was dark in the yacht's hold. Darker than she had ever known it could be. So dark that it seemed to stifle her; a dread, evil, living thing.

Joan's perspiring fingers shook a little as she fumbled with the switch. In an instant, the flashlight flicked on. The sudden yellow beam of light hurt her eyes and made them blink. When she could see, she began to examine the contents of the hold.

There were a dozen or so heavy boxes strewn about the little room. In one corner stood a cluster of shovels, picks, and bars. She moved closer and gasped when she saw the particles of sand that still clung to them.

With a quick glance around the hold, Joan started toward the stairs that led up to the hatch. How she happened to see the little tin box she did not know. It was thrust so far between two cartons that only a narrow sliver of metal could be seen. Her eyes must have caught the gleam of reflected light as she swept the spot with her flashlight. She stopped curiously and moved the beam back to the spot.

Pushing the cartons apart, Joan picked up the box and thrust it into her pocket. A moment later she was approaching the door to their stateroom, half running down the passageway in her haste to get out of sight.

"Joan!" Felicia cried as she threw open the door. Mimi gasped.

"Where have you been?" her friend demanded. "And whatever have you been doing?"

Joan clapped a hand to her mouth in warning.

"Stop shouting," she whispered hoarsely, "and shut the door or we'll have everyone aboard in here!"

Felicia did as she was told, mechanically.

"Now what have you been doing?" she demanded. "And how did you get so dirty?"

Hurriedly she told them all that she had learned.

"I knew something mysterious was going on," Mimi observed. Then her curiosity broke out. "What's in the box?"

Joan fished it from her pocket.

"I don't know if there's anything in it." she replied. "I didn't wait to look inside."

Joan pried the lid from the crudely made tin box.

"Look!" she cried in dismay. "It's only a block of paraffin. And a dirty one at that."

Mimi picked it up and examined it intently.

"There's something pressed into it," she said.

There were two carefully made impressions in the wax.

"We ought to know what that is," Joan said, her forehead wrinkling.

Felicia chewed a stick of gum, pressed it into the indentations, and carefully removed it.

"A key!" Mimi cried.

"And a very special key," Felicia whispered.

"These impressions were made from that twisted key Mr. Chandler always carries!" Joan added.

CHAPTER 6

A SPLASH

Felicia Cartright breathed deeply. Her eyes did not leave the square of paraffin on the table. For a time, she did not move. Then she reached out slowly, as though drawn to it, and touched it with the tip of her forefinger. Her face was white and drawn, and her arm trembled slightly.

"I can't understand this," she whispered. "Why would anyone on board want to make a wax impression of Mr. Chandler's key? Why would he go to all that trouble when he could easily break the lock in the box or locker or whatever it was that the key fit? And how did he manage to get it away from Mr. Chandler long enough to do it?"

Joan tossed her head in a quick, nervous gesture. "The person who made this probably wanted a key so he could open the lock in a hurry without Mr.

Chandler knowing about it," she said. "If the lock were broken, that would give him away."

Felicia examined the impression of the key again. "I wonder how you can tell whether something like this has been used," she murmured to herself. She returned it to the table. "It still doesn't make sense to me," she continued. "The key is so light that it couldn't belong to much of a lock. Why would Mr. Chandler keep anything valuable enough to steal in a box secured with a padlock that could be opened with a sharp, hammer blow?"

"Why would a lot of things happen that have happened on this cruise?" Joan asked laconically.

Mimi Graham had been standing there, wide-eyed, listening. Now she looked from one to the other, searchingly.

"I don't understand what's going on," she said, her voice hoarse and taut. "I don't understand it at all."

"Neither do we," Joan retorted, "to be perfectly frank with you. The only thing I know is that, all of a sudden, I wish we were back at Wellington."

Mimi choked, and her big eyes grew luminous. "I guess it doesn't matter where I am," she said. "It doesn't make any difference at all."

Before either of the girls could reply, they heard footsteps outside their cabin.

"Joan!" Connie called, her voice full of excitement. "Felicia! Mimi! We're ready to go!"

"We'll be out in a minute," Felicia called.

Joan grasped her by the arm. "What'll we do with it?" she whispered.

"Here," Felicia ordered, "put it in the toe of this shoe! I'll stuff it in the back of the closet!"

"Hurry!" Connie cried. She had started back to the upper deck. They could tell by the sound of her voice.

By the time the girls got to the top deck, the launch had already been put into the water. They crawled down to it on a rope ladder.

"This fishing trip had better be good," Joan announced when she got into the gently rolling launch, "after going through *that* to get down here."

"Were you scared?" the first mate asked.

"Scared?" she exploded good-naturedly. "Even my goose bumps had goose bumps."

The wind was lazing in from the east, a faint, half-sleeping wind that wakened now and again to stir the water with one foot.

The first mate cast off the lines that secured them to the *Lori June* and headed the sturdy little launch toward the deep water where the marlin and the sails fed and played tag.

"I'm going to show you girls some fishing that *is* fishing," he said.

"The men fished close by when they were out the other day," Joan told him. "Aren't we going to stay close to the yacht?"

His eyes narrowed.

"I told you I was going to show you some real

fishing," he continued. "The men didn't catch any trophy fish when they were out. In fact, they didn't get anything that was really worth keeping." He drew himself up proudly. "I told them this morning that we were going to start out and keep going until we found something that would open their eyes!"

Joan and Felicia glanced at one another significantly. There could be another reason for wanting them out of the way. Felicia was well aware of that.

"Come on, you two," the mate said, pointing to Connie and Joan. "You'll be the first ones at it." He picked up a hook and started to bait it. "Wish we could fish all four of you at the same time, but the launch is a little small, so we go it by twos."

Felicia and Mimi watched while the sailor rigged the lines and strapped Joan and Connie into chairs at the stern.

"I don't care whether I get a chance to fish or not," Mimi said quietly after a time. "That sort of thing doesn't mean much to me anymore."

Felicia leaned back against the bulkhead and tucked her knees under her chin.

"You sound as though you're carrying the weight of the world on your shoulders."

Mimi picked up a short length of line and fumbled with it uncertainly. "You're not far wrong," she said. "For some reason I feel terribly blue this morning."

The other girl's eyes sought hers.

"You needn't, of course," she said evenly.

Her new friend bristled, "What do you mean?"

"Jesus says, *Come unto me, all you that labor and are heavy laden, and I will give you rest,*" Felicia told her. "If you will only let Him, He will give you the strength you need. He will carry your troubles and sorrows." She paused for a minute. "He has mine."

Mimi faced her, eyes blazing. "You don't know anything about trouble or sorrow either one," she retorted hotly. "You don't know what it's like to lose your mother!"

The silence was long. The only sound was the low, rhythmic drone of the engine, idling at trolling speed.

"I don't know exactly what it's like to lose my mother, Mimi," Felicia said quietly. "But I do know what trouble and sorrow are. Actually, I have never known my father. I can't even remember what he looked like. You see, he died before I was two years old. Mom supported herself and me by doing house-work and cleaning offices. If it wasn't for the help of friends and the scholarships I've been given, I wouldn't even be able to go to Wellington."

Mimi caught her breath sharply. Hurt leaped to replace the anger in her eyes.

"Oh!" she said, her voice faltering. "Oh, I'm sorry!"

Felicia smiled.

"But in spite of that, Mom and I have been very happy," she continued. "You see, we have put our trust in Jesus. That's why I'm so confident that what you need is Christ." She leaned forward earnestly.

"If you confess your sin and put your trust in Him, you'll find that He can lighten the load of sorrow you're trying to carry alone."

Mimi's mouth firmed.

"You sound like Mom," she said cryptically. "Toward the last."

Felicia brightened. "You mean your mom was a Christian?" she echoed. "How wonderful!"

"One of the neighbor women came in and talked with her," she explained woodenly. "Dad and I didn't like it much, but there was nothing we could do about it."

"That changes everything," Felicia told her. "Your mother trusted Christ. That means she is in heaven!"

Mimi turned that over in her mind. "It–" she began uncertainly.

"The important thing now," Felicia said, "is for you to make the same decision. The Bible says that all of us are sinners and worthy of death, but God sent Jesus so we can confess our sin, put our trust in Him, and be saved."

Mimi's throat choked, and she could no longer look at Felicia. She suddenly fastened her interest on a flock of gulls hovering over the placid, subtropical waters.

Felicia Cartright waited prayerfully. She had been talking rapidly up until this point, but now it seemed wiser to remain silent.

"Fish!" Connie shouted. "Fish!"

Almost gratefully, Mimi sprang to her feet and clamored back to the stern to watch Connie Adams battle the wily sailfish. Felicia followed her reluctantly.

That opportunity was lost. Would there be another?

It was an hour later before they boated the magnificent creature and the first mate removed the hook.

"Well?" he asked. The inflection in his voice spoke louder than words. Should he kill the fish to be mounted, or should he return it to the water?

Connie was a moment or two in deciding.

"Let's turn him loose," she said, still breathing heavily from the force of the battle.

The first mate smiled up at her.

"Good girl," he said, and with one quick motion, he picked up the sailfish and dropped it over the side.

They continued to fish for the balance of the day and got several strikes, but no one else actually caught a fish.

"I'm glad you got pictures of it, Felicia," Connie said, her face still flushed with excitement. "I'm afraid that no one will believe me unless I can produce some evidence."

The girl scarcely heard her. Now that they were plowing back toward the *Lori June*, she thought again of the cake of wax secreted in the stateroom. What were they going to do with it?

Mimi must have been thinking of the same thing. She came back to where Felicia was sitting and, looking around, whispered guardedly, "Are we going to give the wax impression of Uncle Norris's key to him?"

"I think we should," and Felicia sighed wearily. If they took it to him, he would have to know where Joan found it and what she was doing down in the hold. He would learn of their suspicions or enough to guess what they were thinking. Still, they had to get the impression of the key to him.

"Maybe we can slip it into his stateroom," she said, "or put it at his table in the dining room in a place where he'll be sure to find it."

There were questions in Mimi's eyes, but she said nothing.

They reached the *Lori June* shortly before dark and went immediately to their cabin.

"The tin box and wax are still here," Joan announced in hushed tones.

"I almost wish they weren't," Felicia said. "Then we wouldn't have to worry about getting rid of them."

Joan took the box and put it in her pocket.

"We can go by the Chandlers' stateroom," she said. "It may be unlocked."

"W-w-what if they catch us?" Felicia asked hesitantly.

"We'll worry about that when it happens."

The girls left their stateroom and started down the narrow passageway together. It was almost dark outside, but the passageway lights had not yet been turned on. They could see along the length of it but indistinctly. It was just dark enough so they could see that the door to the Chandlers' stateroom was slightly ajar.

"Look!" Felicia cried in a thin whisper. "We are in luck."

"S-s-sh! Somebody's in there."

"They won't be paying any attention to the door," Felicia told her. "We can stop for a jiffy, slip it in, and be gone before they know it."

Joan took the little tin box from her pocket with moist fingers. The two almost tiptoed along the passageway. At the door, Joan paused, stooped, and pushed the box of paraffin through the crack of the door. It was done so quickly, so silently, that even Felicia, whose heart had been hammering violently, could scarcely believe it had been accomplished.

Joan grasped her arm and squeezed it lightly.

"Come on," she murmured, "let's get up on deck!"

Halfway up the stairs, Felicia stopped.

"Did you get rid of the box?" she asked.

"Of course, I did," Joan replied. "I–I said I would, didn't I?"

"I was beginning to wonder. It all happened so fast."

"I was wondering too," she went on, "especially when I heard Mr. Chandler cough."

They walked briskly along the top deck to the dining room.

"I'm glad that's gone," Joan Bailey managed. "I'm still shaking!"

Felicia grasped her by the arm. "Look!" she whispered. "I thought you said you heard Mr. Chandler cough! There he is!"

Sure enough! The owner of the yacht and his wife were sitting at their favorite table!

Joan stared.

"But there was someone in the stateroom," she protested. "We both heard him!"

"Let's go back and–" her voice choked off as they heard a door open behind them.

Felicia grasped Joan by the sleeve and quickly pulled her into the shadows with her. A dark, shadowy figure came through the door they had just used. It was a man. They could make out his dark trousers and the dark hat pulled down over his face. But in the semi-darkness, that was all they could see.

Whoever it was paused momentarily and looked around as though trying to learn whether he was being seen. Then he strode quickly to the rail. He drew back his arm and threw something far out into the water.

Felicia Cartright stifled a gasp as she heard the splash. There was no need to have seen what he threw. Instinctively she knew!

The wax impression of the key was gone!

CHAPTER 7

A DARING PLAN

For a long minute, the man at the rail stood there staring out into the darkness. Then he turned and melted back into the shadows.

"He–he's gone!" Joan whispered under her breath.

"And so is that wax impression of Mr. Chandler's key," Felicia replied. She shifted uneasily from one foot to the other. "What are we going to do?" she asked. "We can't just stand out here."

Joan gulped once or twice and straightened with a bravado she did not feel.

"We'll go in there and show them that we're having as much fun as the rest of them," she said. A smile flickered briefly on her lips. "At least we can *act* as though we're having as much fun as the rest of them."

"I'm not even sure I can do that," Felicia told her falteringly. "I'll do well if I get in there at all."

Joan took her arm.

"Come on," she said. "We're not afraid of them."

Together they went through the door. Neither Connie nor Mimi was in the dining hall. The girls looked around momentarily and chose a table nearby.

They thought they had gone into the dining hall unobserved, but the moment they were seated, Phoebe Chandler came over and joined them.

"I–I only want to talk with you a minute," she said, sitting down and leaning forward so she could talk in low tones.

"W-what about?" Felicia asked, her voice betraying her tenseness.

But Mrs. Chandler did not notice.

"It's about Mimi," she said. "What happened today?" The question came out flatly, without emotion.

"Nothing that I know of," Joan said, "but Felicia got to talk with her more than I did."

Phoebe Chandler turned to Felicia. "Come to think of it," she said, "Mimi did mention your name."

She sat quietly and waited. Felicia squirmed uncomfortably, and the color flooded her cheeks.

"Mimi was feeling terribly blue today," the girl went on. "I told her she needn't carry all her burdens alone, that she could turn them over to Jesus as I have done."

Mrs. Chandler's face was grim. "That part of it is all very well," she said, "but what was this talk of sin and being a sinner? She came to me a little while ago asking for a Bible. When I began to question her, she broke down and started to cry. I've never seen anyone so miserable."

There was anger and accusation in her eyes.

"I had to tell her there isn't a thing to the stuff you tried to tell her," she continued, her voice rising harshly. "The idea of a sweet young girl like Mimi crying over her sin. She hasn't committed any sin!"

"The Bible says *all have sinned and come short of the glory of God*," Felicia quoted, "and *all we like sheep have gone astray. We have turned each one to his own way, and the Lord has laid on him the iniquity of us all.*"

Mrs. Chandler got to her feet.

"I much prefer not to think about things like that," she said stiffly. For an instant, she stared down at the girls. "I asked Mrs. Rawlins to bring you along because I thought you would be good for Mimi, that you might be able to help her. I certainly did not expect you to try to make a religious fanatic of her!"

She turned abruptly and walked away.

"Did you hear that?" Joan exclaimed. "Was she mad!"

Felicia took Joan's hand.

"But did you hear what else she said?" she whispered softly. "Mimi is concerned about her sin. That's the reason she was crying! Joan, we've got to talk to her."

"From the looks of Mrs. Eagle Eye across the way," Joan muttered, "we're not going to get the chance tonight. She looks as though she's going to keep Mimi under lock and key."

The girls ate in comparative silence and went below to their stateroom.

"Do you suppose that guy who found the paraffin key impression saw us put it in that stateroom?" Felicia asked. "Do you suppose he knows who did it?"

Joan Bailey started.

"Felicia!" she exclaimed. "You can think of the most horrible things!"

"I thought Connie and Mimi would come in before we finished," Felicia said. "I was hoping we might have a chance to talk with them."

Joan crossed to the porthole and looked out.

"That's strange," she said curiously.

Felicia joined her. "What are you talking about?" she asked. "I don't see anything so different."

"It's probably nothing," she answered, "but I thought we were on the side of the yacht that looked toward shore when we went to dinner. But now that the anchor has been lowered, I see we're on the Gulf side once more."

"That's right!"

Felicia stared out into the darkening twilight. A few moments before, the Gulf was a sparkling blue in the rays of the setting sun, and soaring gulls stood out stark and white against the cobalt sky. But now the sun was at rest. The blue of the water became a dull slate-gray to blend with the drab and colorless sky.

Felicia watched the darkness grow.

"We decided that the noise we heard the other

night was someone lowering a boat over the side, didn't we?"

"That's certainly what it sounded like," her friend replied.

"The fact that they turned the *Lori June* means they're going out tonight," Felicia went on.

"At least that's the logical conclusion."

Felicia Cartright straightened, and her eyes glinted with excitement.

"We'll listen tonight," she said, her voice a thin whisper. "And when we hear the boat go ashore, one of us will swim after them and find out what they're doing!"

Joan Bailey choked.

"You–you're just kidding," she exclaimed. "You don't really mean that. Do you, Felicia?"

She stared at her friend disbelievingly.

"Do you, Felicia?" she repeated.

"I've never been more serious about anything," Felicia went on. She, too, was trembling but for a different reason. "We're only about three or four hundred yards offshore, and there's no moon tonight. There wouldn't be much chance of being seen. If we do that, we can *know* what's going on!"

"It might not do us much good," Joan retorted cryptically, "if we get caught! Did you ever think of that?"

"But I'm not going to get caught," the other girl said. She turned to the closet. "I think I'll get into my swimsuit now."

Joan bristled.

"Oh, no, you're not!" she said. "If anyone's going to–to be silly enough to follow that boat ashore, it's going to be me."

"I thought of it first."

"But I can swim faster than you."

"It's not going to be a race," Felicia whispered, giggling. "All I'm going to do is swim ashore to find out what they're doing."

But Joan was insistent. "If you're going, I'm going too. I'm not going to let you get caught alone."

"There has to be someone aboard," Felicia countered. "I'll swim ashore, and you can stay on deck to help me up when I get back."

"I know how to settle it," Joan said.

She took a length of string, broke it in two, and held it in her hand so that only the two ends showed.

"Now," she whispered, "take your pick. And remember the one who gets the short string wins."

Felicia hesitated momentarily.

"Hurry up," Joan told her. "They might start to lower that boat at any minute."

The Cartright girl reached out and pulled one of the strings from her friend's hand.

"Oh," Joan moaned, "I might have known it! You got the short one."

"What did I tell you?" Felicia replied. "If you'd just have let me go ahead, we could have saved all this time."

Concern twisted Joan's young face.

"Do you really think you ought to go through with it?" she asked.

"Of course, silly," she exclaimed. "Now hand me my suit."

They heard the loud, protesting squeak of a pulley.

Both girls froze.

For a brief instant, it sounded as though it had come from the passageway just outside their stateroom door. Then it came again. This time it was guarded and prolonged, as though someone were striving desperately to keep the noise down.

"They're going ashore!" Felicia managed. "We've got to hurry!"

She slipped into her swimming suit.

"I don't think we ought to go through with it," Joan told her uneasily. "I'd never forgive myself if something happened to you."

"And I'll never forgive you," Felicia said pleasantly, "if you keep me standing here talking until we miss out on everything. Come on, let's go up on deck!"

They were at the stateroom door when they heard the faint splash, as though the boat had been dropped a foot or two into the water. Then all was still, except for their labored breathing.

"You–you will be careful, won't you?" Joan asked desperately.

"Of course," Felicia told her. "Now come on before I–" she gulped hard, "before I lose my nerve."

CHAPTER 8

A LOCKED DOOR

The girls slipped out of the stateroom door into the dark passageway.

"Brrrr," Joan said, shivering. "I get the creeps just being here in the dark. I don't see how-"

Felicia's arms were trembling slightly, and goose flesh roughened her skin.

"Now be sure and stay on deck until I get back, Joan," she said. "And when I whistle to you, lower the rope ladder to me."

"Maybe it's a good thing you're going," the other girl said, laughing silently. "I'd probably have to stay down there. I'd be too scared to whistle."

"Joan Bailey," Felicia exclaimed, "if you don't stop that, you'll have me so I can't do anything!"

"You wouldn't want me to lie, would you?" Joan asked.

"If you can't be cheerful," Felicia countered, "j-just don't say anything."

They got a rope ladder from a chest on the top deck, tied it securely to the railing, and Felicia began to lower herself over the side. She went down confidently, without pausing, until she reached the bottom rung. Then she looked up, waved to Joan, and, relaxing her grip, slipped silently into the warm water.

She had entered the water from the Gulf side of the anchored yacht. That meant she had to swim around the stern of the *Lori June* before heading toward shore.

There was a slight wind blowing. It was not strong, with scarcely body enough to push widely spaced, knee-high breakers up on the gentle slope. But, fortunately, they made noise enough, the muted ruffle of snare drums, as they tasted the gleaming white sand. There was just sound enough to hide the noise of her strokes.

The time waiting on board the *Lori June* had been the worst. Then she had Joan's protests to answer and the doubts those protests raised. There had been too much time to think. But now all that was different. She was busy – doing something.

Logic indicated that the boat that left the *Lori June* at night had headed directly to shore. That was the only explanation for coming back to the same place as they did and for turning so the girls were all on the Gulf side of the anchored yacht, an added precaution against their seeing anything if they looked out of their portholes at the wrong moment.

Felicia swam directly for shore. She moved quietly, effortlessly, through the water, with long, powerful strokes that ate up the distance.

The surf was getting rougher. That meant she was in shallow water very near to shore. She stopped and treaded water, listening intently.

For a time, she heard nothing except the rhythmic sound of the breakers.

For a full minute she listened, straining against the sound of the surf. Then her ears began to filter out a faint digging noise. There was no doubting it! That was the grating of sand against the steel of shovels! Someone was digging on the beach! Out there just beyond her range of vision!

Felicia felt an icy chill. Her heart faltered in its beating.

"I tell you, Doc," someone said edgily, "we're not getting anywhere. Are you sure you haven't made a mistake in locating the spot?"

The digging stopped.

"I tell you I couldn't have made a mistake." The voice was harsh.

It drove like a spear of fire into Felicia's heart. That was Dr. Rawlins on the beach!

"I've checked that map a thousand times," he continued. "It's got to be around here somewhere. If we just keep digging."

"Then why don't we find something?" the other man wanted to know. "It's getting harder all the time to keep it quiet."

"I'm as anxious to wind it up as you are," Dr. Rawlins answered. "Having to hang around this way is going to attract every small-time crook and free loader in the area."

By this time, Felicia Cartright had calmed a little. Straining, she could see a clump of coral a few yards away. It only stood two or three feet above the water, but it was rough and jagged and would offer some protection for her to move closer to the men on the beach.

She paddled stealthily toward it, with only her eyes and the top of her head out of the water.

"If you buried it here, Doc," another voice put in, "someone must have found it and made off with it. After all, it's been eight months."

Felicia quivered with excitement. That was Mr. Chandler! What were they doing?

"I'm not giving up so easily," Dr. Rawlins repeated. "We knew someone might come along and try to find it, so we took real pains to see that it was well hidden."

"You probably didn't do as good a job as you thought you did," Mr. Chandler countered. "Someone has made off with it. If they hadn't, we'd have found it long ago."

"We can't leave until we're sure," the scientist insisted doggedly.

Felicia was close enough now so she could hear the men breathing and see their dark forms against the white sand beach.

"Then let's come out here and do our excavating in the daytime," Chandler went on, "when we can see what we're doing."

"That'll never – wait a minute!" Dr. Rawlins exclaimed, his voice quavering.

"What is it?" Chandler demanded. "Did you find something?"

"I–I'm not sure."

"Here," the third member of their party said, "let me have that shovel!"

Felicia's heart was beating fiercely. She clung to the coral and lifted herself silently, striving to see.

* * *

Back on the deck of the *Lori June*, Joan Bailey glanced quickly around. The yacht was dark except for the running lights and the lights on the bridge. Still Joan was tense and vaguely uneasy.

But there was no one in sight.

Confident that she was not being seen, she knelt to roll up the rope ladder.

"Good evening, Miss Bailey," Captain Adams said pleasantly.

Joan started. Ice water seemed to surge through

her veins, and she began to tremble. Her face was white, she knew, and moist with perspiration.

"I–I–" she stammered, looking up at him. For a moment, she crouched there ridiculously.

"I–"

"Are you a new member of my crew?" he asked, stooping to lift the rope ladder.

"I was just going to put it away," she managed.

"That was thoughtful of you," he said. "I'll do it for you. I suppose someone was negligent in not putting this ladder away."

He coiled the ladder and held it while he talked with her. She rubbed at her throat uneasily.

"I–I can take it below," she said. Somehow, she had to get her hands on that ladder. Felicia would have to have it when she came back aboard.

"No," he replied, his voice pleasant, "I think I will take it with me. I want to show it to the crew tomorrow."

Joan swallowed miserably. What would Felicia do now?

He leaned against the rail and looked out into the darkness.

"There's a certain fascination about this part of the world," he said almost dreamily, "that I've never been able to understand. A person gets to hating it at times, but somehow, it always brings me back. I know now, in spite of all its shortcomings, that I love it down here."

"It is beautiful," Joan said. But her mind was not on the quiet, moonless night nor the sundrenched days. Something had to happen! And soon! She had to get rid of Captain Adams and find something to use as a ladder to help Felicia get back aboard the *Lori June*. If she didn't, her friend would come swimming back to the yacht and signal to her. That would ruin everything!

"If I ever settle down, I believe it will be in this part of the world," the captain went on. "I'd like to build me a little place on an island out here and spend the rest of my days."

"That would be nice," Joan answered absentmindedly. It would be nice, too, to have him out of the way so she could help Felicia get back on the *Lori June*. She had to get rid of him somehow.

While she was still casting desperately for a way of getting Captain Adams to leave her alone on deck, he looked at his watch.

"Say," he exclaimed, "it's getting awfully late, and I've had a big day today." He yawned deeply. "I think I'll be turning in."

In the darkness, she knew that he was eyeing her intently.

"How about you?" He asked the question pointedly.

"I think I'll go down to my cabin too," Joan said quickly. "We've been planning on going fishing tomorrow."

"Now that is a good idea," Captain Adams said.

"It's a good idea to go down to your cabin and go to bed, and it's a good idea to go fishing tomorrow."

He took her gently by the arm and guided her toward the door that led to the staterooms on the deck below.

"We'll see you in the morning."

"Good night," Joan told him.

She would have protested, but she could not. There was something so deliberate, so straightforward and purposeful in his manner. She went into her cabin and closed the door.

On the other side of her stateroom door, Joan Bailey paused thoughtfully.

"Joan," she said to herself, "if we didn't know Captain Adams better, we'd be sure that he was giving us the brush-off."

For several minutes, she waited in the darkness until she was sure that the captain of the yacht had gone to his own stateroom. Then she tiptoed to the door and quietly turned the knob!

Her mouth dropped open and her lithe body stiffened!

The door was locked!

She could not get out! And Felicia would be swimming back to the *Lori June* at any minute!

CHAPTER 9

FOOTPRINTS!

While Felicia had been crouching fearfully behind the clump of coral, the wind pushed the last remnants of clouds away. They were thin, wispy clouds with little substance or body, but they had served to keep the night as dark as indigo. Once they were gone, there was a thin sliver of moon a few degrees above the horizon and a double handful of stars scattered aimlessly about the sky.

The light they gave was feeble, like so many tiny candles, but they served to soften the heavy blackness of the night. Felicia could see the drooping palm fronds against the sky and could separate the figures of the men crouched tensely around the hole they were digging on the beach.

Although they had not looked her way, the faint light seemed to be directed squarely at her. She loosened her grip on the coral and dropped lower in the water.

"Hurry up!" Dr. Rawlins exclaimed.

"Here!" The digging stopped. "If I'm not digging fast enough for you, here's the shovel!"

Felicia saw one man clamber out of the hole and the other enter. Then the digging began again at a furious pace.

For several minutes, the measured, rhythmic sound of sand against the steel of the spade continued. Then there was a dull thud. Though she was more than a dozen yards away, Felicia could hear it plainly.

Silence gripped the little group.

"W-w-what was that?" Mr. Chandler demanded.

"Get the flashlight!" That was Dr. Rawlins, but his voice was so pinched and thin it scarcely sounded like him.

The flashlight went on suddenly with a burst of light. Felicia started and ducked as Chandler swept the beam in an arc above her head. For the space of a heartbeat, she froze, terrified.

"We've found it!" Dr. Rawlins shouted exultantly. "We've found it!"

The rays of the flashlight were almost completely buried in the hole. They reflected off the white sand and cast eerie shadows on the faces of the men. Felicia summoned all her strength and raised herself above the piece of coral. But she could see nothing.

"Look at it!" the scientist cried. "Isn't it magnificent?"

"Well, come on!" Mr. Chandler broke in, his manner tense. "We've got to get back to the *Lori June* and get under way."

"You mean we're going to leave tonight?" the third member of the party asked. "What are the others going to think?"

"We'll tell them something," Mr. Chandler retorted. "We've got to get out of here. And the sooner the better."

"That's right," the scientist echoed. "There are men who wouldn't hesitate to kill if they knew the value of what we've got here."

For an instant or two, Felicia clung there, unable to move.

What was it they had found? Why was it so valuable? And why had they been so secretive? The questions came, but there were no answers. A deep, nameless dread welled within her, and suddenly she could not get back to the yacht too soon.

The full import of what she had heard soaked into her consciousness. The boat would be heading back to the gleaming white yacht. And quickly! And, as soon as it was aboard, she would be weighing anchor and pulling away! Felicia had to get back before they did!

She loosened her grip on the coral, gave a powerful push with her feet, and began to swim through the surf toward the yacht. She swam silently, but with a certain desperation that gave an extra surge of power to each stroke and kick. She swam faster than ever before. Yet it seemed as though she were scarcely moving.

Fortunately, the moonlight reflected off the white of the *Lori June* to make a clearly visible target. Felicia swam to her quickly.

The boat was in the water now. She could hear the splashing of the oars. It was a good thing she and Joan had lowered the ladder from the Gulf side of the yacht. She would surely be seen trying to go up the side that was visible from the dory.

She swam around the stern and along the *Lori June* to the place where Joan would be waiting. She was breathing heavily and was trembling with excitement. In another minute she would be aboard and down in the safety of their stateroom once more.

The nearness of the yacht and the safety it represented seemed to sap her strength. She stopped short.

The ladder! It was gone!

Felicia whistled guardedly and waited. The only sound was that of waves lapping lazily against the steel hull.

"Joan!" she cried inwardly. "Where are you? Where are you?"

There was no answer to her whistle.

Frantically, Felicia glanced along the sleek, white yacht. Their stateroom was on a lower deck, but the porthole was much too high for her to reach. And, even if she could reach it, it was much too small for her to wriggle in. For a brief instant, panic seized her.

"O God," she prayed, "You are the only One who can help me. Help me to attract Joan's attention or do something to get back on board before they start to move!"

Perhaps Joan had misunderstood where they were to meet. Felicia was waiting on the Gulf side of the *Lori June* while Joan was waiting on the other. Quickly she kicked herself away from the hull and swam around the stern anchor chain.

The dory was coming now. She knew that, although she could not hear the oars. That realization almost panicked her.

Felicia reached a spot comparable to that where she had first gone on the other side of the yacht and whistled.

Again, there was no answer.

Something had happened! There was something wrong! Joan Bailey would be out there to help her if she possibly could!

Felicia could hear the squeak of the leathers and the splashing of the oars in the water. That meant the little boat was drawing close to the *Lori June*. Whatever she did, she had to do quickly.

She swam to the stern of the yacht and started to go around it when she saw the anchor chain again. She looked up at it.

It wouldn't be easy, but there just might be a chance of–. She placed her hands on the coarse chain and began to climb, digging her bare toes into the links for support. It was a difficult, exhausting climb, but Felicia reached the railing in a moment or two and pulled herself over it. She clung there momentarily, panting heavily.

Almost at the instant she reached the deck, she heard the sound of a winch at the opposite end of the *Lori June*. It squeaked now and again, defiantly, as though daring the men who were operating it to be quiet.

"Take it easy, you guys," a voice muttered hoarsely. "You'll have everyone on board awake."

Breathlessly, Felicia got to her feet and crept along the deck, pressing against the superstructure. She had to move in their direction in order to reach the door that led to the deck below. She did so stealthily, her heart scarcely beating.

"Well," Mr. Chandler said, his voice lowered, "you got what you came after, Rawlins. Are you satisfied now?"

"I will be," the scientist said, "when we get this thing safely into the United States."

Felicia fled down to the lower deck. As she did so she heard Dr. Rawlins say, "Where are you going, Chandler?"

"To rout out Captain Adams. We're getting under way."

There was a sound on the stairs. Felicia stopped in the passageway and pressed herself against a cabin door. It was unlocked, and she eased herself quickly into it.

"Did you see anything?" a voice asked from just outside the stateroom door. It was a tense, excited voice, and for that reason was probably a bit louder than the speaker had intended. To Felicia, who was crouched on the other side of the door, the voice boomed. It was the third man of the party.

"Not a thing," someone else answered. That was the first mate.

She glanced down at the crack at the bottom of the door. A narrow yellow wedge of light revealed the fact that one of the men carried a flashlight.

"We've looked everywhere. We must have been mistaken."

"I tell you there's something fishy," the other said, dropping his voice to a coarse whisper. "That girl's greasy footprint couldn't possibly have been made this afternoon."

Felicia started! She might have known there was grease on that chain! And plenty of it! She had left footprints! Her throat contracted suddenly. That would guide the men right to her!

"What makes you so sure?" the man asked.

"Captain Adams had men out scrubbing down the decks this afternoon. If those footprints were there then, they would have been scrubbed away."

"Maybe they missed the footprints," the first mate

replied. "It's happened before when we don't have inspection after the job's been done."

"It's too bad she didn't get a little more grease on her feet. We could have trailed her where she was going. That way we'd have found out who she was."

"You can stand here all night if you want to," the yacht's first officer said. "I'm going to turn in."

In a moment, the passageway was quiet.

Felicia waited a moment or two, then slipped out of the empty cabin and stole quietly toward the door of her stateroom.

As she approached it, the door opened stealthily and Joan stepped out.

"Joan!" Felicia gasped.

"Felicia! Am I glad to see you!"

She closed the door behind them and bolted it.

"I–I've been frantic," Joan continued. She told Felicia how Captain Adams had come out on deck and how she had gone to their cabin thinking she would sneak back out in a moment or two. "But the door was locked!" she exclaimed. "There wasn't anything I could do!"

Felicia gasped. "That was close!" she exclaimed.

While they were talking in whispers, the engines of the *Lori June* began to hum.

"We're getting under way!" Joan said.

Felicia breathed heavily. She wiped her moist face with a towel.

She dropped the towel and straightened.

"I just thought of something. I left greasy foot-prints all over the deck!"

"Oh, Felicia!" Joan cried. "In the morning, they'll go nosing around a little more and will see that they are your footprints. You're the only one aboard with such small feet!"

For a long minute, Felicia did not answer. "I know," she said at last. "Get me your bar of soap and a dirty blouse."

She got her own raincoat, made a crude water bag by tying the sleeves, and filled it with water.

"Here's the blouse and the soap," her roommate replied, "but I still don't see–"

Felicia left the stateroom, glancing nervously up and down the passageway. Now that the yacht was moving, members of the crew would be on deck. She would have to be careful. Very careful. Joan was right behind her.

Hurriedly they found the footprints, scrubbed them away, and slipped back to the stateroom.

"Do you think we were seen?" Felicia whispered.

"Here," Joan said, taking the dirty blouse and shoving it out the porthole.

"Wait a minute!" Felicia said, grasping for it. "That was a new blouse of mine."

"It's gone now," Joan answered. "No one is going to find any evidence in here."

"If I'd known that," Felicia told her, "I'd have made you get one of your own blouses."

The girls slept little that night and were up shortly after dawn, dressed, and waiting for breakfast.

"I wish that clock would get a move on," Joan said. "I'm getting awfully hungry."

"So am I, but I don't know whether I'll be able to go in and face Mr. Chandler and Dr. Rawlins after all that happened last night."

"I can," Joan retorted, "if I've got to do it in order to eat. I'm starved."

At last, the breakfast hour came, and they left their stateroom and made their way up to the dining room.

"Oh, there you are!" Mimi called to them brightly as they entered the door. "We've just been talking about you."

Felicia felt her cheeks tinge delicately.

"I hope it was good," she replied as she and Joan approached the table.

On other occasions the passengers aboard the yacht had ignored the big table in the center and used the little tables around the sides, but this morning everyone was sitting at the big table.

"We were just talking about a real mystery," Dr. Rawlins said, glancing first at Felicia and then Joan.

"There's probably a logical enough explanation," Mr. Chandler put in, "but it's a mystery to us, isn't it, Franklin?"

The men laughed, but it seemed to Felicia that their laughter was edged and calculated, as though it were part of some act the men were putting on.

"Yes," the owner of the yacht said, "the deck of the *Lori June* was thoroughly scrubbed yesterday afternoon, and last night the first officer and one of the crew found a pair of girl's footprints at the stern."

"And barefooted at that," Dr. Rawlins added.

"I still don't see how they could have gotten there," Connie said. "They would have dried in no time."

"Not these footprints," the scientist went on. "They were in grease."

"Of course," Mr. Chandler said, "they weren't actually footprints. They were really just toe prints."

"That doesn't seem like much of a mystery," Joan said depreciatingly, as though where she came from, they found strange footprints a couple of times a week.

"That isn't the whole score," Dr. Rawlins said. "We were out at dawn this morning to check them, but they were gone! Vanished!"

Mimi and Connie laughed. Felicia and Joan joined them, hoping that it sounded realistic.

CHAPTER 10

A STALLED ENGINE

Felicia Cartright and Joan finished breakfast as quickly as they could and excused themselves.

"Don't forget," Dr. Rawlins called after them, "we want you on deck in a little while. We're going to have a lot of fun today."

"We'll be there," Joan told him, laughing frivolously as though she had nothing else on her mind. "Be sure and call us when you're ready."

"Will do."

The girls went back to their stateroom.

"What do you suppose is happening to him that he's getting so nice all of a sudden?" Joan asked when they were alone together.

Felicia checked the lock on the door, almost fearfully, and when she spoke, her voice was scarcely more than a whisper. "Do you suppose he wants to be nice?" she asked. "Or is he interested in having us where he can watch us?"

Joan's dark eyes widened.

"Felicia Cartright!" she exclaimed. "You can think of the most awful things!"

"I can't help it," Felicia answered. "I get goose bumps every time I think about the things that have happened on this trip."

"And we still don't know what they came down here for," Joan said, "or what they found."

The girls were still talking guardedly when there was a sharp knock at the door. They both jumped at the sound and stared at one another.

"W-w-who is it?" Felicia asked, stammering a little.

"It's only me."

"Why, that's Mimi!" she said under her breath.

Joan walked briskly to the door and opened it. "Come on in."

Mimi entered the room and looked from one to the other quizzically. "What's the matter with you two?" she asked.

Felicia smiled sheepishly. "You startled us."

Mimi turned to Joan almost abruptly. "Dr. Rawlins sent me down after you," she said. "He's about ready to get a game going on deck, and he needs you to fill in."

Joan paused at the mirror and fluffed at her hair with her fingers, almost subconsciously.

"You're coming too, aren't you?"

"We'll be up in a few minutes," Mimi explained. "Tell them to play the first game without us."

Joan looked at her curiously. "Okay," she said. "I'll be seeing you."

Mimi followed her to the door and closed it deliberately. It was almost a minute before she turned. It seemed to Felicia that her entire manner changed. The lines around her mouth softened, and her lips trembled slightly. She swallowed hard, as though there was a lump in her throat that would not be put down.

"I must talk with you," she said. She spoke softly enough, but her voice was as taut as a tight-wire and edged with emotion.

Felicia waited.

"Aunt Phoebe says I'm crazy to listen to you and your fanatical religion," she blurted.

Felicia's expression was still soft and concerned.

"And what do *you* think?" she asked gently.

Mimi moistened her lips in a quick, nervous gesture.

"I–I don't know," she said. "I don't know what to think."

They sat down on the side of the bed, and Felicia got her Bible.

"What I say doesn't mean anything, Mimi," she began. "I could easily be mistaken. And so could your Aunt Phoebe. The only thing that really counts is what God says about it in His Word."

She turned to the second chapter of 1 Corinthians and read: "*But the natural man receives not the things of the Spirit of God: for they are foolishness to him.*"

There was no sound in the little stateroom except Mimi's heavy breathing.

Felicia flipped the pages back to the book of Romans.

"And here is the spiritual truth that verse talks about," she went on. "*If you shall confess with your mouth the Lord Jesus, and shall believe in your heart that God has raised him from the dead, you shall be saved. For with the heart man believes unto righteousness; and with the mouth confession is made unto salvation.*"

Mimi's face was pale, and she was working her moist hands slowly.

"I read those verses this afternoon," she said. "I didn't understand what they meant."

Felicia started at the beginning and explained the way of salvation. How she needed to realize that she was a sinner and in need of a Savior. And how she had to put her trust in Jesus Christ to save her from the result of her sin.

Mimi listened eagerly, and, in a few minutes, knelt beside the bed with Felicia to confess her sin and put her trust in Christ.

It was almost an hour later when she and Felicia finally went up on deck.

"There you are," Joan sang out when she saw

them. "It took you so long that I was about to give up hope. Thought you had fallen overboard, and the sharks had eaten you."

Everyone laughed except Mimi.

"No," she said, her voice ringing loud and clear and with a resonance Felicia had never heard in it before, "but the most wonderful thing has happened to me. I've confessed my sin and put my trust in Jesus. I'm a Christian now!"

Phoebe Chandler, who was sitting in a deck chair nearby, dropped her book and gasped. Her face went white, and something akin to shock and anger stood in her eyes.

"I see now," Mimi went on, "what I've been missing all these years."

"Now that is something," Phoebe exclaimed, her voice brittle. "Little Mimi, a plaster saint."

"Aunt Phoebe," the girl said, her eyes full of tears, "don't make fun of me."

"That's right," Mr. Chandler broke in firmly. "Don't make fun of her, Phoebe. She may have something we all ought to have."

Someone changed the subject and soon the game started again, but it was a listless, half-hearted game. And before it was half finished, they quit and went to the lounge or their staterooms.

"Oh, Felicia," Joan said as they walked along the passageway to their stateroom, "I had no idea that Mimi was so close to accepting Christ!"

"Neither did I. In fact, I almost didn't witness to her at all. She seemed to be so distant, so far away from spiritual things."

That afternoon Dr. Rawlins worked doggedly at keeping the games going. They played up until dinner time and finished in the lounge that evening. Some of the games had been strenuous, and when bedtime came, both Felicia and Joan were exhausted. They had devotions with Mimi, who stopped by their stateroom for that purpose, and went directly to bed.

"I do declare," Joan began, "from everything that's been going on I don't think I'll ever be able to sleep until we get back on shore again."

Felicia only heard the first sentence or so before she drifted off to sleep.

It must have been hours later that she awakened suddenly. She sat straight up in bed. Darkness was all around her. A thick, impenetrable curtain of black that shut out everything and gave her the strange feeling of living in a void.

All was silent. There was no sound anywhere. Still, fright gripped her with icy fingers, and she realized that she was trembling violently. Something was wrong! That was sure! Her mind, still fogged with sleep, struggled to understand. Was there someone in the room? Were there strange sounds that had woken her? Sounds that ceased the instant she stirred?

Was – Could there be someone in the room? She almost screamed.

And then understanding began to soak into her consciousness. It was not noise that had wakened her, but the lack of noise. Silence! The engines of the *Lori June* had stopped suddenly and without warning.

She got up and tiptoed to the twin bed where Joan lay sleeping.

"Wake up," she said, shaking her friend. "Joan, wake up!"

The girl stirred restlessly and brushed Felicia's hand away.

"Wake up!" the Cartright girl exclaimed, shaking her again.

Joan opened her eyes and stared at Felicia in the darkness.

"W-w-what's the matter?" she asked, stammering. "It's not morning yet. It–it's still dark."

"I know that. There's something wrong with the yacht."

Joan threw her feet across the edge of the bed and sat up.

"Are–are you sure?" she demanded.

"Listen for yourself," Felicia retorted. "The engines aren't running."

Joan Bailey was sitting motionlessly on the side of the bed. An instant before she had been sleeping soundly. Now she was still half-drugged. She blinked her eyes and rubbed them with her small fist.

"Joan!" Felicia said, raising her voice and shaking

her friend once more. "Do you hear me? Are you awake?"

"I–I think so," Joan replied numbly. There was a brief pause. "You said something about somebody running, didn't you? Why would anyone want to run in the middle of the night? And why would you want to get me up to watch them? Sounds silly to me."

Felicia had already gotten into a robe and slippers. "Come on," she said, "I'm going to see what's wrong."

By this time, Joan was wide awake. "Oh, no, you don't! You're not going to get away from me."

She put on her robe, and they went out into the passageway together.

"What's wrong?" she whispered.

"That's what I want to find out," Felicia said. "The yacht's engines stopped a few minutes ago."

When they reached the top deck, they saw Dr. Rawlins and Mr. Chandler standing there, talking in low tones.

"There's nothing for any of us to worry about," Mr. Chandler told them. "We'll be under way soon."

"But what made the engines stop like that?" Felicia insisted.

It seemed to take a long while for either of the men to speak, and when they did so, their manner was evasive.

"Captain Adams has everything well in hand," the yacht owner said. "Now I would firmly suggest that you girls go back to your stateroom and get some sleep."

"T-t-thank you," Joan managed.

But they did not go below immediately. They were still standing there when another figure approached them in the darkness.

"Oh, it's you!" Connie said.

"What are you doing up?" Felicia wanted to know. "It's the middle of the night."

"I'm as curious as you are," she replied. "I wanted to find out what was happening."

"So do we," Joan said, "but we haven't been able to find out a thing."

"It's really nothing serious," Connie told them. "Some sort of engine trouble. Dad got the chief engineer out, and he's working on it now. I think he'll have us under way in a little while."

The girls talked with her for a moment or two and went back to their stateroom.

"We could just as well have stayed in bed," Joan said, switching on the light.

Felicia did not answer her. She began to move, almost mechanically, around their stateroom.

"Joan," she gasped, "someone has been in here!"

"Felicia Cartright! Don't scare me like that! I've gone through enough for one night."

"But it's true!" Felicia repeated. "Look! My suitcase was pushed up against the bulkhead, and now it's not!"

Joan's face went white.

For a minute or two they looked around the room in silence.

Joan was the one who spied it.

"Felicia!" she cried tensely. Her finger wavered as she pointed. "Look!"

There on the floor lay a small, badly twisted key! The key Mr. Chandler always carried!

CHAPTER II

THE KEY FITS!

Felicia Cartright picked up the key gingerly and began to examine it.

"It's Mr. Chandler's," Joan whispered hoarsely. "How do you suppose it got in here?"

Felicia turned it thoughtfully between her fingers. "That's his key," she said. "I'd know it anywhere. But we saw him up on deck, so he couldn't have dropped it in here."

"He could have given it to someone else," Joan suggested.

"Or," Felicia added, "it could have been made from the wax impression we found."

Joan Bailey gave a startled cry.

"I'd never thought of that!" she exclaimed. "Do you suppose it could be?"

"It doesn't belong to us," Felicia replied, examining the key intently, "and it wasn't here when we left a few minutes ago. That means it belongs to somebody who knew we were on deck."

Joan expelled her breath slowly.

"Felicia," she said, "I'm getting so I don't like it here. Let's go home!"

"I'm almost beginning to wish we could," she answered.

Felicia took a ring of keys from the dresser and compared them with the key they had found on the floor.

"This doesn't look like much of a key," she said. "It isn't heavy enough to lock much of a door."

"That's what I was thinking," Joan answered. She took the key and stared at it. "It probably fits a small box or some sort of a locker."

She moved closer to the light. "I thought probably I could tell whether this is the new key or not," she said, "but I can't be sure." She glanced up. "You know, Felicia," she continued slowly as though making a most important discovery, "somebody brought this key in here."

"A startling deduction," Felicia retorted, laughing. "With a detective like you, we'll have this case solved in no time."

"I'm serious," Joan said. "Somebody brought this key in here, so it's probably safe to assume that he did so because he planned to use it."

"Now we are getting at the heart of the matter!"

Felicia said, her eyes dancing as she needled her best friend. "Your intellect overwhelms me!"

"It does?" Joan murmured. "I didn't even know that I had one. Now to get back to this key. There must be some sort of lock in our stateroom that this key would unlock. That must be the reason they broke in here."

Felicia took the key again.

"There's either a lock in here that this key fits or they had a good reason to think it's here."

"So you finally see what I'm talking about?" Joan asked triumphantly, walking about the stateroom. "Now what is there in here that this key fits?"

"We've got most of the keys that operate the locks in this cabin," Felicia replied. The small locker above the closet caught her eye. "We don't have the key for that one, do we?"

"The steward told us it was full of bedding and we wouldn't be needing it."

Felicia stood on a chair and tried the key in the lock.

"Does it work?" Joan demanded excitedly.

The other girl shook her head.

They were so concerned about the key that they did not hear the footsteps in the passageway. Indeed, they had been so excited to learn that someone had entered their room while they were on deck that they had forgotten to lock the door. Now it opened noisily.

"Oh!" Felicia gasped, almost falling off the chair.

"Don't get so excited," the newcomer said. "It's only Mimi."

The girls turned, weakly, to face her.

"D-d-don't do that," Joan managed. "You c-c-could have caused us to have heart attacks. Especially me."

"I'm sorry," Mimi told them. "I was up on deck to see why the yacht stopped, and when I came back, I saw the light under your door. I should have knocked."

"That's all right," Felicia replied, her face twisting into a smile, "but let's get the door locked so we don't have any more unexpected visitors. They might not turn out to be so nice."

Mimi looked from Felicia to Joan and back again.

"I've got to know something," she said. "What's going on here?"

"That's what we'd like to know," Joan answered.

"You won't say anything to anyone about what we tell you, will you?" Felicia asked.

"Not if you don't want me to. But what is going on? Why is everyone so mysterious?"

"Wait a minute," Joan said, moving quietly to the bulkhead and switching off the light. "If you saw the light under our door, Mimi, so could someone else. And that's just what I don't want. More visitors."

"But I don't see–" Mimi protested.

"You will," Joan answered confidently. "You will."

Starting at the beginning, Felicia told her everything.

"And now," she concluded, "we found this little

key in our stateroom. It's your uncle's or one just like his."

Before Mimi could speak, they heard a muffled footstep in the passageway outside their stateroom. The girls stiffened, scarcely daring to breathe.

"Where did you have it last?" a gruff voice asked guardedly.

"I remember having it when I tried the locker in this cabin," the other said, "but I'm sure I put it back in my pocket."

"If you'd put it in your pocket, it would still be there," the other retorted irritably. "Now you've just about ruined everything!"

"But I tell you, boss," the other replied, "I've had a lot of things on my mind tonight. I had to get in touch with you by radio and get the *Lori June* stopped just where you wanted her. I had to help you sneak aboard and–"

"But you should have found out where they have hidden it. Now we've got to search the whole yacht."

"I did the best I could. I found out that the only safe place aboard was the ship's safe. I'd have found out where it's located if anyone knew. Chandler is the only one who knows where it is, and he's not telling."

The other man muttered something under his breath.

"And," the crew member went on, "I stole Chandler's key to it and made a wax impression of it–"

"And now you've lost the key!" They were moving

on slowly, but the girls could still hear enough of their conversation to make out what they were saying. "We're going to have to work fast, or the whole deal will be ruined!"

"We should have jumped them in Guatemala like I said," he went on defensively. "The cops wouldn't have done anything to us if they had caught us. Old Rawlins was just as illegal as you and I."

The men passed on out of hearing.

For a long minute, no one moved. The men had spoken in such hushed tones that it scarcely seemed real to Felicia now that they were gone. It was just a dream, embroidered from fear and an overactive imagination. It couldn't be anything more.

But Joan thrust out a clammy hand and clutched her wrist tightly.

"W-w-what are we going to do?" she asked. Her lips scarcely moved, and Felicia had to guess the words.

It was Mimi who first spoke audibly. "Did you hear what they said?" she asked, desperation edging her voice. "Dr. Rawlins and Uncle Norris have been doing something crooked! I can scarcely believe it. They've always been so nice."

Felicia moistened her lips.

"There–there might be some explanation," she said weakly. But there was no conviction in her words.

"W-w-what should we do?" Joan asked again. "There are a couple of thieves loose aboard."

"M-maybe we'd better go to Mr. Chandler," Felicia suggested. "He ought to know about those two men."

"Go to him?" Joan echoed. "How can we without giving away what we know?"

"I don't see–" Felicia began, but her friend broke in quickly.

"What would he do if he knew that we've found out about him and Dr. Rawlins?" she asked, shuddering. "You can go and tell him if you want to, but I'm not going to risk it!"

"But we've got to trust somebody," Felicia said. "We can't handle this ourselves."

"We could go to Captain Adams," Mimi put in. "We know that we can trust him."

Joan shook her head.

"Oh, no! He's the one who made me go to my room the night you swam ashore, Felicia. He's the one who locked me in there. If there's anything going on, he's in with Dr. Rawlins and Mr. Chandler."

Felicia brushed her hair from her eyes nervously.

"The first mate seemed like an honest guy," she said. "I believe we could trust him."

Joan thought for a moment. "I'm not sure," she countered, "but I suppose we would come as close to depending on him as we could anyone else on board."

"What would we tell him?" Mimi asked. "He might go right to Captain Adams or Uncle Norris himself."

Felicia nodded her agreement, although it was so

dark in the stateroom, she could only vaguely make out her two companions.

"I suppose you're right," she said. "If we could show him some evidence though. Something real that would make him see there is reason to be concerned, I'm sure he would help us."

"Like what?" Joan asked laconically.

"We've got the key to the ship's safe," Felicia said. "If we could locate it and find out what it is they've stolen, we would have something to talk with the first mate about."

"What good would that do?" Mimi asked. Her hands were working nervously.

"He could get the radio operator," Joan answered, "or operate the radio himself and get help from the authorities on shore. They could come out with a helicopter or a rowboat or something."

"I don't know," Mimi said, her voice numb. "I still can't make myself believe that Uncle Norris would get involved in anything crooked. Why should he? He's got more money than he would ever want."

"Maybe when we find out what it is that has been stolen," Felicia said, "we will have the answer to a lot of questions."

"So," Joan said with mock resignation, "all we've got to do is duck those two characters who were just outside our door, find the safe, and hope that this key opens it."

"Before those men do it for us," Felicia added cautiously.

Joan got to her feet.

"I don't know why I run around with you, Felicia," she said. "Every time I do, we get into trouble."

Mimi Graham sighed miserably.

"This is one of the worst experiences of my life," she said again. "To think that Uncle Norris is a–a crook."

"No, Mimi," Felicia told her, "don't even think that until we find out all the story."

"But everything points that way," the girl countered, "even though I can't believe it."

Felicia patted her comfortingly on the shoulder.

"If we've got to do this," Joan broke in, "let's get with it. Now where would we be apt to find that safe?"

"It's not in the lounge or one of the public rooms," Felicia said. "Those guys would already have given them a good going over. And they haven't found what they're looking for."

"It probably wouldn't be out like that anyway," Joan said. "And it wouldn't be in the crew's quarters or the captain's stateroom."

Felicia took her hand from Mimi's shoulder.

"It's the sort of thing that would be used by the owner of a yacht, isn't it?" she asked.

"That means the chances are it would be in the master stateroom that Mr. and Mrs. Chandler are using."

"That sounds logical enough," Joan said, "but those men would have thought of that too. Wouldn't they have already broken in there to look for it?"

Mimi drew in her breath sharply. "You–you aren't saying that we ought to break into their stateroom, are you?" she asked tremulously.

"Of course not," Joan Bailey told her. "If it had been in there, one or the other of those men would have found it. That only leaves the staterooms, the galley, the radio room, and places like that."

Mimi pursed her lips.

"It seems as though I remember something about that safe," she said. "It was way back when I was a little girl, right after Uncle Norris bought the *Lori June*. The yacht belonged to someone else before he got her, you know."

"But what about the safe?" Joan asked insistently.

"I'm trying to think," she said slowly. "Uncle Norris was taking us through the yacht for the first time when he took us into a small stateroom."

"The safe," Joan said again, "you've got me biting my fingernails. What about the safe?"

"I'm coming to that," Mimi continued. "He said the owner of the yacht was a peculiar man who had taken this little cabin for himself. Then he touched a button, and a panel opened to show this safe."

Felicia gasped.

"I just remembered something!" Mimi cried.

"That funny, little twisted key he is always fooling with unlocks it!"

"That's it!" Felicia said excitedly. "It has to be!"

"Now," Mimi said, "all we've got to do is find that stateroom."

"It's probably in the Rawlinses' stateroom," Felicia said in dismay. "That would be the logical place."

"But they have the other suite," Mimi countered. "This was just a small stateroom, like this one."

"Do you suppose it could be here?" Felicia asked.

Mimi jumped to her feet.

"I know!" she exclaimed. "I just remembered! It's in the stateroom across from you!"

"Are you sure?" Felicia persisted.

"I remember it distinctly now. I don't know why it didn't come to me before."

Joan started for the door.

"Let's go!" she exclaimed. "What are we waiting for?"

They opened the door and stole silently across the passageway and into the cabin. Their hearts were hammering furiously, and their breathing was in short, thin gasps.

"I hope this doesn't take long," Joan said to no one in particular as she threw the night latch to lock the stateroom door. "I don't much care for it."

"Now the safe was over here behind this panel," Mimi whispered. "I remember it as plain as though he showed it to me this afternoon."

She fumbled momentarily hunting for the release, and Felicia and Joan waited fearfully. But in an instant or two, the panel swung open to reveal a large, old-fashioned safe.

"That's it!" Joan whispered tensely.

Felicia's fingers were trembling so that she could scarcely insert the key in the lock.

"I've never seen a safe that was opened with a key before," Joan observed.

The tumblers fell into place as she turned the key, and the safe door opened.

"Ah!" Felicia managed.

At that very instant, there was the sound of footsteps at the door.

"Somebody's coming!" Joan gasped.

Paralyzed with fear, the girls crouched on the floor before the safe.

"The door's locked," a hoarse voice whispered.

"Just a minute. I've got a skeleton key here somewhere!"

CHAPTER 12

THE CUT ROPE LADDER

For an instant or two, the girls did not move.

"O God," Felicia prayed silently, "You have helped us so many times when we've called on You. We don't deserve it, but please help us and keep us safe!"

While she was still praying, she remembered the door that led into the adjoining stateroom.

"O God, help it to be unlocked!"

She was already on her feet and tiptoeing toward the door.

"Felicia!" Joan whispered. "Come back here!"

She turned the doorknob. There was a loud, protesting squeak, and the door opened.

In spite of herself, Joan screamed.

"Pete!" a voice outside exclaimed softly. "There's someone in there! Hurry up!"

"Come on!" Felicia ordered in low tones.

Mimi and Joan scrambled to their feet and dashed toward the door, slamming it behind them. In one motion, Joan turned and flicked the night lock.

An instant later, the men burst into the empty stateroom.

"They went into the next cabin," the one called Pete whispered guardedly. "I'll get 'em!"

"Wait a minute!" the other said. "They found the safe, and there's the key in the door!"

"We've got to get out of here!" Joan said tensely.

The girls crept to the door that opened into the passageway, slipped out and into their own stateroom.

"Now we've ruined everything!" Felicia said.

Joan locked the door.

"We've got to be quiet," she cautioned. "They've got a skeleton key. They can come in here too if they happen to want to."

"Joan," Felicia said, "we've got to do something! We can't let them get away with this!"

"But what can we do?" Her voice was desperate.

Mimi went to the porthole and was looking outside dejectedly.

"Girls!" she cried moments later. "There's the getaway launch! It's right outside the stateroom!" They crowded close to her, staring at the launch that was secured to the deck of the *Lori June* by a long line.

"If we could just reach that rope," Joan said, "and cut it, those guys couldn't get off the boat." She stopped suddenly. "What am I saying? Who wants to keep them on here?"

"Maybe we can't reach it from here," Felicia said. She opened one of her bags hurriedly and got the knife that belonged to her deep sea-diving outfit.

"What are you going to do?" Joan and Mimi both demanded.

"I'm going up and cut that line!"

Before they could protest, she opened the door and stepped out into the passageway.

Had she been a moment sooner, she would have made it. As it was, she got to the stairs when the men came out of the stateroom and saw her.

"There's one of them!" Pete cried, his voice soft but commanding. "Stop! Stop, I say!"

She dashed up the stairs, but before she reached the top, he grabbed her by the arm.

"Now, my little lassie," he cried angrily, "maybe you'll learn not to stick your nose into things that don't concern you."

"Ouch!" she protested. "You're hurting me!"

"I'll hurt you worse than that," he promised, "if you let out a peep. Now get up on deck and be quick about it. And remember! Don't do anything that will attract the attention of the night watch."

"Here," his companion said, "take this a minute, Pete, and whatever you do, don't drop it. I want to make sure she doesn't yell."

"What are we going to do with her?"

"Take her along. There's nothing else we can do."

Felicia held the knife tightly at her side.

The tall, swarthy man pushed a clean handkerchief into her mouth and tied it in place with another one.

"Now get a move on!" he whispered.

He pushed Felicia ahead of him across the deck. There wasn't time to be frightened. She breathed a prayer silently.

"Now climb down that rope ladder, and be quick about it," the man ordered.

Felicia glanced up at Pete. He was the steward who had waited on them! He was holding a strange, stone figure in his arms. It was old and very hideous, unlike anything she had ever seen before.

"Do as I say!"

She crawled over the rail and sought the rope ladder with her feet. In the excitement and darkness, they had not thought to search her. She still held the knife in her hand.

Felicia went down the ladder slowly. There had to be something she could do to get away!

She glanced up to see Pete start after her.

That was it!

Instantly the plan came to her. Stooping hurriedly, she cut the rope ladder just below her feet, cut it so that only a strand held. Then she dropped the knife, kicked herself away from the *Lori June,* and dived!

"Let her go, Pete!" the other man whispered in warning.

But by that time Pete stepped beyond the cut in the rope ladder. It gave way without warning, plunging him into the water. He screamed loudly.

Felicia let herself go deeply into the warm water. She was free! Thank God, she was free! Free!

Felicia loosened the gag on her mouth and swam under water along the side of the *Lori June*. Now all she had to do was stay out of Pete's way for a few minutes.

When she surfaced, all was excitement aboard the yacht. The lights were on, and men were running in every direction. The searchlights switched on and began to sweep the water around the anchored ship.

"Man overboard!" someone shouted hoarsely. "Man overboard!"

That would be Pete, Felicia realized. No one knew as yet that she was in the water. No one, that was, except Pete and his companion. She swam leisurely into the beam of one of the searchlights.

"There's a girl out there!" a man's voice cried.

Moments later, they threw her a life ring, and she was pulled to a hastily lowered rope ladder.

"Felicia," Joan called out from the railing above her, "are you all right?"

"Of–of course!"

She had been calm enough all the time she was in the water, but now as she began to climb to the deck of the *Lori June*, the strength went out of her legs and arms, and she began to shake violently. Her body ached, and it seemed a big effort even to lift a foot from one rung to the other. She paused shakily, clinging to the ropes on either side.

Captain Adams saw that she was in trouble.

"Get another ladder over the side," he ordered crisply. "And you, sailor, go down and help her aboard."

Knowing that help was coming seemed to give Felicia new strength and courage. She moved up another rung and another. By the time the sailor came running back with the ladder, her fingers reached over the gunwales.

"Now!" Captain Adams said, grasping her wrists in his own iron grasp. "You're safe aboard!"

The first mate came over and gave him a hand. Felicia crawled weakly over the railing, almost collapsing as she did so.

"Are you all right?" Mimi asked tensely. "We've been praying for you ever since you left us."

Felicia managed a smile.

Someone helped her across the deck to a chair. She had not realized that almost everyone aboard was crowded around her until she brushed the hair from her eyes and looked up.

"Is she all right?" Mr. Chandler asked, concern in his voice.

Captain Adams nodded. "She's a little tired. That's all."

Then she remembered the men.

"Where are they?" she demanded. "Did they get away?"

"We've got them safely below," the captain said. "And that's where they're going to stay until we get ashore where we can turn them over to the authorities."

"And we got the jeweled goddess," Dr. Rawlins said. "We have you to thank for that."

Felicia's eyes widened. "But it went into the water with Pete, didn't it?" she asked.

"No," Dr. Rawlins said. "His companion didn't trust him to carry it down the ladder, so he still had it in his arms when a couple of the crew grabbed him."

"I'm all right," she protested. But they insisted on putting a blanket around her shoulders.

"I suppose you'd like to see what caused all the trouble," the scientist went on. He held up the ugly, stone figure a foot or so high. Its eyes were dull, green stones, and there was a necklace of exquisitely shaped green stones about its neck. Even through the grime of centuries, it was easy to see that they were valuable.

"Emeralds!" Dr. Rawlins exclaimed. "A small fortune in matched emeralds!"

Felicia stiffened and looked away. A nameless dread took hold of her.

"Of course, we wanted it for its archaeological value. It is absolutely priceless."

Mr. Chandler joined them just then.

"This thing is beginning to make sense," he said crisply. "Pete is one of the two new crew members who were hired the day we sailed. He and his pal beat up our two regular stewards so they could get him planted aboard."

"I thought there was something strange about the guy," Dr. Rawlins replied. "I didn't trust Pete from the start."

"And," the yacht owner went on, "he finally told us where he had the radio transmitter we spent so much time looking for. That's how he contacted Brad Joslin, and the two of them made plans to stop the yacht so Brad could come aboard by launch."

"They would have gotten away with it, too," Dr. Rawlins said again, "if it hadn't been for Felicia and her friends."

"What we want to know," Joan blurted, "is what's been going on here? What were you doing? And why were you so secretive?"

Dr. Rawlins paused momentarily. His face grew serious.

Joan and Felicia both stared at him intently.

"It wasn't our idea," he said firmly. "I can assure you."

Connie and Mimi moved closer, listening almost breathlessly.

"We came down here about six months ago," he began, "under an arrangement with the government of Guatemala that they were to get half of any artifacts we found. We got this object and half a dozen others as the result of a month's work. The other things were of about equal value to this piece. But in view of the fact that we had nothing like this in our museum, we decided on it."

"Then you didn't steal it!" Mimi exclaimed, relief evident in her voice.

"Is that what you thought?" Norris Chandler broke in. "I could see that you have been acting strangely the past few days. I just thought it was that fanatical new religion you're so excited about."

"My faith in Jesus has changed me," she acknowledged, "but we've been terribly concerned about what was going on. We thought maybe you were doing something that might get all of us into jail."

"I know we were acting strangely," Dr. Rawlins said, "but we were about to be jumped by bandits six months ago when I buried the artifact hurriedly and made a crude map. Somehow Brad Joslin had gotten word that we'd found something of value and was going to get it from us. He had about a dozen hired thugs with him, and we didn't dare try to slip it past them.

"We planned to come back and get it," he continued, "but they stayed around so long that we went back home and left it buried there."

"But why did you have to keep it from us?" Felicia asked. "Didn't you trust us?"

"It wasn't that at all," Norris Chandler added. "Doc, here, knew how clever Joslin is. He wouldn't dare show himself aboard because Doc had seen him, but there was a good chance that he'd have a spy aboard the *Lori June*. And it turned out that he did. That was the reason we couldn't risk letting anyone else know about it. We didn't even tell our wives."

Felicia and Joan and Mimi looked at one another, relief evident in their faces.

"Norris!" Mrs. Chandler said abruptly. "Do you realize that poor girl is still in wet clothing? She'll catch pneumonia."

"I feel all right," Felicia protested. "Honestly, I do. The water was so warm."

"Wet clothes are uncomfortable," Mimi's aunt said. "Wouldn't you like to go down and change?"

Joan and Connie and Mimi went below with her.

"I don't know whether I'll ever be able to sleep again," Joan said.

"I'm so thankful that Uncle Norris and Aunt Phoebe aren't involved in anything crooked," Mimi put in. "You have no idea how terrible that made me feel."

Felicia changed clothes quickly.

"I suppose we ought to go to bed and try to get some sleep," she said, "but I certainly don't feel like it."

Connie, who had been strangely quiet since they entered the stateroom, turned to Mimi suddenly.

"You said something to your uncle a little while ago," she began. "Something that I didn't get."

"What was that?"

"He mentioned some 'fanatical' religion," Connie said.

Mimi nodded.

"And you said that your faith had made you different. What were you talking about?"

Mimi Graham took a minute or two to answer. "You know how miserable I've been on this voyage. It didn't seem to me that life was even worth living. And then Felicia and Joan started talking with me."

"About what?" Connie asked curiously.

"About confessing my sin and trusting Jesus Christ as my Savior."

There was a short, poignant silence.

"I suppose you'll think I'm awfully dumb," Connie went on, "but I don't even know what you're talking about."

Mimi started at the beginning and explained the way of salvation haltingly, step by step.

When she finished, Connie was visibly affected.

"I–I'll have to do some thinking about that," she said hesitatingly, getting to her feet. "Maybe we can talk more about it tomorrow."

"We'll be praying for you," Mimi said, her eyes revealing her concern.

Felicia and Joan both nodded their agreement.

"It's the most wonderful thing in the world," Felicia said.

THE
FELICIA CARTRIGHT SERIES

Felicia Cartright, a petite blonde who is one of the most popular students at Wellington School for Girls, has a surprising inclination toward mysteries. If a mysterious situation arises, it either makes its way to Felicia, or Felicia somehow finds it. Though this is a bit trying for her happy-go-lucky roommate, Joan Bailey, it does prevent life from becoming monotonous. It also enables Bernard Palmer, the popular author of the "Danny Orlis" books, to write an entertaining series of stories for girls aged twelve to eighteen.

The mysteries range from a valuable missing antique to an attempt by claim jumpers to steal a deposit of tungsten ore. There's excitement and action galore—but there's also spiritual guidance and blessing because Felicia and her partner-in-adventure love the Lord and take Him into account in all their experiences.

AVAILABLE FROM WWW.ANEKOPRESS.COM